DOCUMENTARY FILMMAKING FOR ARCHAEOLOGISTS

To my son, Joseph Pepe, a trusted friend and confidant,
a great teacher, and an outstanding husband and father.

—Peter Pepe

To the two most important people in my life,
my adoring wife, Pat Meaney, and
my lovely goddaughter, Lisa Randesi.
Both inspire me.

—Joseph W. Zarzynski

DOCUMENTARY FILMMAKING FOR ARCHAEOLOGISTS

PETER PEPE AND JOSEPH W. ZARZYNSKI

Left Coast
Press Inc.

Walnut Creek, California

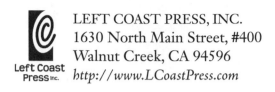

LEFT COAST PRESS, INC.
1630 North Main Street, #400
Walnut Creek, CA 94596
http://www.LCoastPress.com

ISBN 978-1-61132-201-9 hardback
ISBN 978-1-61132-202-6 paperback
ISBN 978-1-61132-203-3 institutional eBook
ISBN 978-1-61132-686-4 consumer eBook

Library of Congress Cataloging-in-Publication Data:
Pepe, Peter, 1952-
   Documentary filmmaking for archaeologists / Peter Pepe and Joseph W. Zarzynski.
      pages cm
   Includes bibliographical references and index.
   ISBN 978-1-61132-201-9 (hardback : alkaline paper)
   — ISBN 978-1-61132-202-6 (paperback : alkaline paper)
   — ISBN (invalid) 978-1-61132-203-3 (institutional ebook)
   — ISBN (invalid) 978-1-61132-686-4 (consumer ebook)
   1. Motion pictures in archaeology. 2. Archaeology—Methodology. 3. Documentary
films—Production and direction. I. Zarzynski, Joseph W. II. Title.
   CC85.P47 2012
   070.1'8--dc23
                              201203751
Printed in the United States of America

♾ The paper used in this publication meets the minimum requirements of American
National Standard for Information Sciences—Permanence of Paper for Printed
Library Materials, ANSI/NISO Z39.48–1992.

CONTENTS

ILLUSTRATIONS

ACKNOWLEDGMENTS

THIS BOOK IS AN OUTGROWTH OF a workshop that we first taught in January 2008 at the Society for Historical Archaeology's 41st Annual Conference on Historical and Underwater Archaeology held in Albuquerque, New Mexico. Entitled "An Archaeologist's Guide to Documentary Filmmaking," the one-day workshop was well received, and we have held it at several other Society for Historical Archaeology (SHA) annual conferences and at other venues, too. Without that initial SHA workshop, this book probably would not have come into being. So, we want to thank Karen Hutchinson, Executive Director for the SHA, and our initial SHA workshop coordinator, Jamie C. Brandon, an archaeologist and anthropologist at Southern Arkansas University. Both had the vision to accept our workshop proposal.

Furthermore, this book would not have been possible without the patience, enthusiasm, and understanding of our publisher, Mitch Allen. Mitch is a regular attendee at major archaeology and anthropology conferences around the country. At these conferences, he can generally be found in the conference book room where he both promotes the science of archaeology and displays the many fine books that his company publishes. When we first proposed our book idea to him, he promptly opened up a line of communication that we often exercised, and which culminated in Mitch offering us the book deal. It has been a pleasure working with him and his talented staff at Left Coast Press, Inc.

There are several other people that need to be acknowledged, too. Joseph Pepe, Peter's son and business partner at Pepe Productions, is an enthusiastic member of the digital natives of the world, and thus he clearly understands the magnitude of the digital revolution and the emergence of social media as a means to promote the genre of documentary filmmaking. Joseph frequently shares his vast knowledge of video filmmaking and website design which we put to excellent use when writing those sections in our book. John Whitesel, a dear friend and an incredible animator and computer technician, also provided valuable information, about the somewhat esoteric world of computer animation. Unfortunately, the week before the initial draft of this book went to Left Coast Press, Inc., John passed away from cancer. His animation and computer-generated images have imbued our archaeology documentaries with a *tour de force* quality that has been one of the hallmarks of Pepe Productions videos. Our thanks likewise go out to Kathleen McCormick, a consummate museum collections manager at the St. Augustine Lighthouse & Museum (St. Augustine, Florida), and her husband, Doug Bowen, an old-school animator and artist. The couple loaned us several books on Eadweard Muybridge, Winsor McCay, and the history of animation that we consulted frequently when researching our book. James P. Delgado, a NOAA underwater archaeologist and administrator, kindly provided us with detailed information on the television series, *The Sea Hunters*, which we included in our book. Vincent J. Capone (Black Laser Learning), a side-scan sonar specialist who uses video productions to teach his highly technical craft, shared his expertise in producing training DVDs on remote sensing, which we described in one chapter in the book. We also want to thank Lori Toledo and Pat Meaney for being our sounding boards throughout this endeavor; Pat likewise was helpful doing some fact checking for us. Thanks are due as well to all the groups and individuals that were supportive of our underwater archaeology documentaries. These include Bateaux Below, Inc. (Russell P. Bellico, Bob Benway, Vincent J. Capone, Terry Crandall, and John Farrell), the Lighthouse Archaeological Maritime Program (Chuck Meide, Samuel Turner, Brendan Burke, Christine Mavrick, and Starr Cox), the Wiawaka Holiday House staff, the Fund for Lake George, Inc., the *Lake George Mirror* (Lake George, New York), *The Chronicle* (Glens Falls, New York), *The Saratogian* (Saratoga Springs, New York), the *Glens Falls Post-Star* (Glens Falls, New York), the *Albany Times Union* (Albany, New York), *The Daily Gazette* (Schenectady, New York), Kip Grant, Kathy Abbass, Sam Bowser, Steven C. Resler, Paul Cornell, Mark L. Peckham, Alan Bauder, Christina Rieth, Charles Vandrei, John Wimbush, David Starbuck, Garry Kozak, Martin Klein, Ralph Wilbanks, Clive Cussler, Elizabeth Miller, Kathy Fleming (St. Augustine Lighthouse & Museum), the 2009 Lighthouse Archaeological Maritime Program Field School, Lisa and Tony Hall, Paul Post, Chris Carola, and Lee Coleman. Furthermore, we wish to thank those people who provided the images used in this book and who are duly credited in the photo captions. Also, we appreciate the work of Mitch Allen and Julie M. Schablitsky for their review and comments on the manuscript of this book. Finally, we would be remiss if we did not thank the numerous people who purchased our underwater archaeology-related DVD documentaries and also those folks who viewed the productions during public screenings. In so doing, they gave us confidence in our documentarian skills that eventually translated into our writing of this book.

INTRODUCTION

"A story is not a story until the story is told."
—Vincent J. Capone (Black Laser Learning)

A LMOST ALL VETERAN ARCHAEOLOGISTS, regardless of their research focus, have been told at least once in their professional careers, "Your archaeology project would make a great **documentary**."* Those commentators were probably correct, too. Across the full range of projects, from investigating an eighteenth-century battlefield in upstate New York, to mapping a War of 1812 shipwreck in Lake Ontario, to excavating an Anasazi village in New Mexico, conducting a palynology analysis of a postglacial pollen core from Ireland, or using aerial photography to search for ancient Roman camps in Britain, most archaeologists have noteworthy and fascinating projects that beg to be interpreted and told in a variety of ways.

More often than not, archaeologists convey the results of their studies by formal reports, professional papers, public lectures, and articles in popular publications or on websites. Seldom does a documentary filmmaker pound on an archaeologist's office door with an interest in making a documentary on the archaeologist's research project unless it is a topic that is highly newsworthy—a recently uncovered pirate shipwreck, for instance, or something sensational like new archaeological discoveries of cannibalism at the 1846–1847 Donner Party site in the Sierra Nevadas. By the same token, most archaeologists lack the knowledge of how to go about finding an accomplished documentary filmmaker to collaborate with on a documentary-style production for release on television, to be sold as a **DVD**,* for use in a museum exhibit, or for dissemination over the Internet.

At its heart, documentary filmmaking—the art of creating a nonfiction film, video, or television program chronicling an event, people, or person—is

---

Documentary Filmmaking for Archaeologists, by Peter Pepe and Joseph W. Zarzynski, 11–16. © 2012 Left Coast Press, Inc. All rights reserved.

* Words set in bold type are defined in the book's Glossary at the end of this book.

all about powerful and emotional storytelling. Documentary filmmaker Sheila Curran Bernard wrote in her book *Documentary Storytelling: Making Stronger and More Dramatic Nonfiction Films* that "[a] good documentary confounds our expectations, pushes boundaries, and takes us into worlds—both literal worlds and worlds of ideas—that we did not anticipate entering" (Bernard 2007:3–4).

Our book is designed to give the archaeologist the necessary knowledge not only to approach a documentary filmmaker or television **producer** or **director** to try to form a working relationship, but also to provide archaeologists with a basic skill set to better understand the documentary filmmaking process. Then, the archaeologist/**documentarian** partnership can become a "well-oiled machine." That said, this book is not designed to suddenly transform the archaeologist into a professional documentary filmmaker. Rather, its intent is to give archaeologists—and, for that matter, other social scientists interested in documentary filmmaking—the awareness and confidence needed to approach documentarians and television producers and directors to join together to create an award-winning documentary or documentary-style television program.

This book shows how archaeologists can form and mold their documentary idea and then proceed through the various steps toward teaming up with an experienced documentarian to create a documentary. We offer tips on writing a proposal, creating a **treatment,** and understanding all the other stages of the documentary filmmaking process. The book's glossary will be extremely valuable for familiarizing archaeologists with the vocabulary used by documentary filmmakers. *Documentary Filmmaking for Archaeologists* reviews the history of documentaries and television and outlines the various types of archaeology- and history-related documentary styles. We also give insight into the **YouTube** phenomenon and describe working on mini-documentaries for screening in museums and even for training purposes. Finally, the book has invaluable information on documentary production stages and suggestions for promoting one's documentary. After reading this book, archaeologists will have a strong knowledge base to successfully team up with a documentary filmmaker to collaborate on their own archaeological documentary.

We are an experienced and professional documentary filmmaking team, having released three feature-length archaeology-related documentaries over a five-and-one-half-year time span. Peter Pepe and his son, Joseph, own and operate a corporate and documentary video production company located in Glens Falls, New York. In 1978, Peter entered the video production field, and two years later, he founded Glens Falls Television Productions, Inc., which today does business as Pepe Productions. Since then, Peter has traveled around the country and overseas, too, producing a vast variety of video productions, including award-winning documentaries. Joseph W. Zarzynski is an underwater archaeologist who serves as the executive director of Bateaux Below, Inc., a not-for-profit corporation that from 1987 to 2011 studied historic shipwrecks at Lake George, New York. In 1993, Zarzynski's group worked with state and local officials at Lake George to open the Empire State's first shipwreck park for scuba divers called Submerged Heritage Preserves. From 1993 to 2011, Zarzynski was part of the coalition of cultural resource managers that jointly administered this shipwreck preserve system. Moreover, Bateaux Below collaborated with the New York State Office of Parks, Recreation and Historic Preservation to nominate and get listed to the National Register of Historic Places several Lake George shipwrecks.

Our archaeologist/documentary filmmaker partnership evolved slowly, taking nearly a decade and a half between our first meeting in 1990 until we finally formed a cooperative team in 2004 (Figure I.1) to start production on a documentary, *The Lost Radeau: North America's Oldest Intact Warship*. That documentary tells the story of a little-known but extremely important historic French and Indian War shipwreck in Lake George called the 1758 *Land Tortoise* radeau (a "radeau" is a simply constructed vessel used most often as a naval battle platform) and dramatizes the underwater archaeological investigation of this one-of-a-kind British and provincial warship that is now a National Historic Landmark. The release of the documentary in 2005 was in large part due to the intervention of animator John Whitescl, who in 2004, fourteen years after Zarzynski originally suggested the documentary to Peter Pepe, proposed the idea to Pepe Productions. Had Zarzynski and his underwater archaeological squad been more knowledgeable and savvy about documentary filmmaking back in 1990, that initial proposal to form a archaeologist/documentarian partnership to produce the 1758 *Land Tortoise* radeau shipwreck documentary most likely would have been accomplished years earlier than its ultimate release date in 2005.

Documentaries are undoubtedly one of the best means for archaeologists or cultural resource managers to inform the public about their archaeology projects. Unfortunately, sometimes archaeologists fall a bit short when it comes to disseminating the results of their research. It has been estimated that up to 60 percent of modern archaeological excavations remain unpublished ten years after fieldwork has concluded (Renfrew and Bahn 1998:535). It is a common refrain within the archaeological community that because the excavation process itself (which is, of course, the fundamental method of collecting archaeological

Figure I.1: The archaeologist/documentary filmmaker collaborative team, underwater archaeologist Joseph W. Zarzynski *(seated left)* and Peter Pepe *(seated right)*, collecting B-roll video footage at an archaeological dig by the Community Archaeology Program, Schenectady County Community College in Schenectady, New York *(credit: Louise A. Basa)*.

data) is destructive by its very nature, archaeologists have even a greater professional responsibility to report the results of their field research and to do so in a variety of ways to maximize the dissemination of that information to the professional and lay communities. Undoubtedly, the type of public outreach project that reaches the largest number of people and that also has the greatest potential to inform with that special "wow factor" is the documentary film genre.

Likewise, the **digital revolution** that has swept through much of the world has created high-quality, lower-budget filmmaking technology. This provides a greater opportunity for archaeologists and other social scientists to seek out documentary filmmakers with whom they can work to produce sensational archaeology- and other social sciences-related "**docs**." And yet, while technology today has made it possible to shoot and edit low-budget documentaries, most archaeologists still seem somewhat reluctant to actively pursue collaboration with documentary filmmakers. This is surprising, given that documentarians are always in search of colossal stories to tell. In general, most archaeologists are passive at best in trying to get a documentary produced about their research project. Too often, archaeologists wait for Ken Burns or one of his documentary filmmaking colleagues to knock on their office door.

So, whether the goal is to create a well-financed, full-feature documentary for broadcast on the History Channel, to make a DVD documentary to be sold in a museum gift shop, to fashion a short, tightly crafted video to be posted on YouTube, to have a professional-looking video to enhance one's website, or simply to gather great video footage for PowerPoint or Keynote presentations, this book shall be your guide.

We literally grew up in front of the **small screen** (television). For the past few decades, and even more so today with the worldwide use of the Internet, this visual and audio medium of documentaries has entertained us, informed us, and permitted us to explore exotic places we could only dream of visiting. So, where are you, as archaeologists, in this process? You could well be an integral component of a documentary filmmaking team. After all, who better than the project archaeologist knows the subject content of archaeological research? A documentary should challenge its viewers and engage them with dramatic emotion and factual accuracy. It can be a powerful educational tool. We two authors have learned documentary filmmaking by doing, by having many successes and a few stumbles along the way, too. We hope this book will help you to tell your magnificent stories in a most compelling manner, as a documentary production.

1
FORMING THE ARCHAEOLOGIST/ DOCUMENTARY FILMMAKER TEAM

The Archaeologist/Documentary Filmmaker Paradigm

A DOCUMENTARY FILM IS A STORY that has found its storyteller. Several years ago, documentary filmmaker Professor Pat Aufderheide (American University) astutely wrote, "I believe the role of the film-maker will be increasingly to work in collaborative partnerships with people who have great stories to tell, passionate convictions, [and] in-side access" (Aufderheide 2006:14). The archaeologist/documentary filmmaker paradigm certainly seems like a natural fit!

Documentaries are truthful stories about people, places, events, and things. A successful documentary is an exposition that is as compelling as it is factual. The documentary filmmaking crew creates a story with a noteworthy beginning, a dynamic middle that includes some twists and turns, and then a satisfying ending (Bernard 2011:2–3).

A documentary is not an exercise of parading one "**talking head**" after another in front of the camera. Barry Hampe, in his book *Making Documentary Films and Videos: A Practical Guide to Planning, Filming, and*

Editing Documentaries, insists that a documentary is a "presentation of evidence—the truth" and functions primarily as a visual argument (Hampe 2007:13). The partnership of the archaeologist and the documentary filmmaker helps to ensure that the subject matter is portrayed accurately and that a proper balance is achieved utilizing the visual argument integrated with interviews and narration.

Most documentary filmmakers, whether employed by network or cable television firms or simply affiliated with local independent video companies, have a primary drive: they want intriguing stories to broadcast! Most documentarians will tell you they also want to be challenged, to be involved in a project that will engage them, one that is exhilarating and will motivate them to do something extraordinary.

There are many kinds of documentary filmmakers with whom an archaeologist might pursue a collaboration. Some documentarians work for large production houses and may have some other type of funding as well, whether from commissioning stations, government agencies, foundations, or corporations. They may even have a technical support team. Others are independent filmmakers who have to be really creative to secure a contract to produce a film. Regardless, practically all documentarians look for terrific stories that have national or international impact (Bernard 2011:7) (Figure 1.1). Their goal might be for a **theatrical release** such as Werner Herzog's 2007 documentary, *Encounters at the End of the World*, about those dedicated scientists who conduct their research in the harsh environment of Antarctica, or his 2010 **3-D documentary**, *Cave of the Forgotten Dreams*, about the Chauvet-Pont-d'Arc Cave art of southern France that dates back over 30,000 years ago (Figure 1.2). Other big-time filmmakers seek to have their documentaries broadcast on network or cable television, such as Spike Lee's 2006 HBO-released documentary about Hurricane Katrina called *When the Levees Broke: A Requiem in Four Acts*. **Independent filmmakers** frequently conduct their work to reach regional and local audiences. Like internationally and nationally esteemed documentarians, independent documentary filmmakers strive for awards and other critical acclaim at **film festivals** held around the country and the world. An emerging outlet for documentary filmmakers is through YouTube and other sites on the Internet (Bernard 2011:7).

Sometimes, an independent documentary filmmaker or a staff member of a production company working for a television network

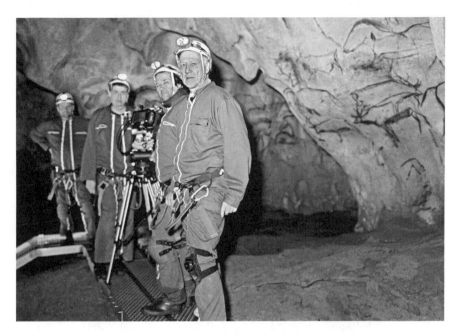

Figure 1.1: Award-winning documentarian Werner Herzog with Peter Zeitlinger and documentary film crew with rock art during the production of the documentary *Cave of Forgotten Dreams* (credit: Marc Valasella & Creative Differences).

might approach an archaeologist about collaborating on a documentary or television production. David Starbuck, an archaeology professor at Plymouth State College in New Hampshire, specializes in eighteenth-century battlefield sites in the northeast United States. He has worked with the History Channel, The Learning Channel's *Archaeology* series, and National Geographic Channel on several archaeology television productions. Starbuck says, "A number of producers learned about our work because of an Associated Press release that was printed across the country" (personal communication, 2012). Television production companies likewise approached him following the publication of a magazine article on one of his archaeological excavations: "All of the programs in The Learning Channel's *Archaeology* series (which aired in 1993, 1994, and 1995) were based on articles that first appeared in *Archaeology* magazine. So each of these shows was based on separate articles that I had published in the magazine. The show's producer, New Dominion Pictures, was put in touch with me by the editor of the magazine" (personal communication, 2012). Thus, getting the word out

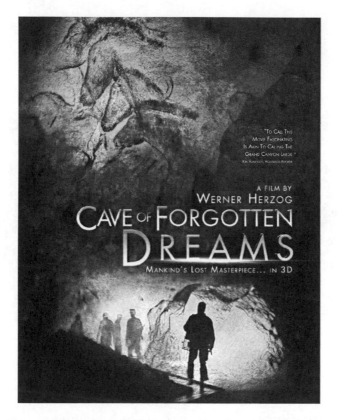

Figure 1.2: One of the most talked about archaeology-related documentaries in years is Werner Herzog's production *Cave of Forgotten Dreams*, a 3-D documentary (*credit: courtesy of Sundance Selects*).

about an archaeology project and establishing oneself as the expert on that topic certainly helps in attracting documentary filmmakers and television production companies. "If you have an interesting story to share, public audiences absolutely love joining with you in the thrill of discovery," says Starbuck (personal communication, 2012).

Pursuing the Documentary Filmmaker

So, archaeologists can sit around waiting for a television production company to contact them, or those with a first-rate story just waiting to be told can actively pursue a documentarian or television production firm for a collaborative endeavor.

How does one chase down a documentary filmmaker? If you are looking for an independent filmmaker from your geographical area, there are numerous ways to find one. Start by checking the Internet via a Google search, or go old-school and consult the Yellow Pages in your local phone book for video production companies. Find local or regional film festivals and then attend one or two of them. Most film festivals have a documentary category, and frequently they feature regionally produced documentaries. Watch a few, and if you find a documentary style you really like, contact the film festival to hunt down that documentarian whose work you enjoyed. Many larger cities also have **film forums** which host monthly screenings of films. Visit your local film forum and absorb as much as you can. Who knows, you might meet some local film aficionados who can direct you to a documentary filmmaker living near you.

You might also want to visit and even join **Withoutabox**, a website devoted to helping filmmakers submit their movies and documentaries to film festivals in the United States and elsewhere. It was founded in 2000. In 2008, IMDb, a division of Amazon, acquired Withoutabox. You can become a member of Withoutabox (there is no cost to register) and thus uncover more information about what film festivals may be located near you. The website allows you to search over 3,000 film festivals worldwide. Members can also sign up to receive e-mail notices on upcoming film festival entry due dates and other relevant film festival information. Though this website is primarily used by filmmakers, it is nevertheless a very useful tool for anyone interested in documentary filmmaking.

You can also seek out local corporate video production companies that make television commercials or video productions for websites. They have the technical skills to make a documentary, but possibly are never approached to do so.

If you want to find an established documentarian, consult the **International Documentary Association** website (www.documentary. org). The IDA is a not-for-profit corporation that was established in 1982 to support programs for documentary filmmaking. They have a wonderful quarterly magazine and an awards program for documentaries. By perusing their website, you may find a documentarian who would be open to a documentary project partnership.

Most community colleges teach a basic course in filmmaking or video editing. These colleges might have a filmmaking club and may even have a campus television studio. Find your local community college and check its website. It's not uncommon to find a wealth of filmmaking talent on a community college campus. Any of these folks might like to partner with you to produce a short documentary on your local archaeology project.

If you locate a local video production company, you really need to unearth a little information about the firm before contacting them. What is the core of their business? Do they have up-to-date video cameras and computer editing equipment as well as experienced personnel with sufficient computer editing skills to complete a documentary?

Once you find your documentarian, you should set up a meeting. Before you meet, you should develop your **pitch** to the documentary filmmaker (see Chapter 8). In preparation, view as many different types of documentaries as possible to get a general understanding of the kind of documentary styles that communicate information and are also sterling storytelling vehicles.

When you find a corporate video or documentary filmmaker, you will need to craft a well-written but short letter, essentially a **tease**. There is no standard tease letter, but we can give you some general hints to help you in drafting that all-important letter. This is the beginning of the all-important relationship. Be direct. Tell the filmmaker you are interested in collaborating on making a documentary about one of your archaeology projects. Briefly cite your professional credentials and convince the filmmaker you are an authority on that topic and that you desire to work with the filmmaker in a collaborative project. Be ready with a catchy title for your documentary, too, and provide the gist of your documentary story in a couple of sentences. Do not overwhelm the filmmaker with details. Just provide a tease. Ask to set up an appointment. You can send your tease letter by U.S. mail or e-mail. If needed, follow up your letter with a telephone call. Remember, when you approach the filmmaker, you are starting a relationship to pique his or her interest. The documentarian wants to know that the archaeologist is well respected, knowledgeable in his or her field, and, if possible, is one of the experts on that subject.

Before we move on to suggestions for developing your formal pitch to a documentarian, the next chapter provides a little background on the history of documentary filmmaking. It will give you a sense of how and when documentaries started.

2
A BRIEF HISTORY OF THE DOCUMENTARY FILM GENRE

I N CHAPTER 1, WE GAVE A BRIEF DEFINITION of the word "documentary." It is now time to describe the word in greater detail, give a brief history of filmmaking development, outline the history of documentary films, and review the introduction of television, since it is one of the prime conveyers of documentaries.

What a Documentary Is

Simply stated, documentaries are truthful stories about people, places, events, and things set in the past or present. Before the advent of television and video, documentaries were called "documentary films" because they were shot on **film stock**, the medium of that earlier time. Today the term "documentary" is more often used to describe the genre.

Archaeology documentaries are essentially stories about the past and the people who lived during the event or time being documented. Many Americans are intrigued about history and about the science of archaeology, too. Thus, it should not be surprising that Hollywood also has a love affair with the past. According to archaeologist Vergil E. Noble, who wrote a section in the 2007 book *Box Office Archaeology: Refining Hollywood's Portrayals of the Past* (edited by Julie M. Schablitsky), of the movies produced in the twenty-five-year period from 1981 to 2006,

Documentary Filmmaking for Archaeologists, by Peter Pepe and Joseph W. Zarzynski, 23–30. © 2012 Left Coast Press, Inc. All rights reserved.

more than half of the 125 films nominated for an Oscar for Best Picture were set in a time before the present. Those Hollywood blockbusters covered periods from the Roman Empire to the Vietnam War (Noble 2007:226). Yes, you certainly could say that Americans do love movies and documentaries about yesteryear.

It is believed that the word "documentary" was coined by John Grierson (1898–1972), a Scotsman who wrote a review of Robert J. Flaherty's film about Polynesia called *Moana*. Grierson's review was published in the *New York Sun* newspaper on February 8, 1926, under Grierson's pen name at the time, "The Moviegoer." In his review, Grierson wrote, "Of course *Moana*, being a visual account of events in the daily life of a Polynesian youth and his family, has documentary value." The term soon caught on to describe nonfictional films. John Grierson would go on to a notable career in documentary filmmaking. He helped to create the National Film Board of Canada, and sometimes he is referred to as the "father of British and Canadian documentary film" (Fulford 2000).

The Development of the Documentary Genre

Long before documentaries hit the **big screen**, however, film, the initial medium of the documentary genre, was developed. The first device that showed animated pictures—let's call them early motion pictures—was a **zoopraxiscope**, because its dynamics were commonly referred to as the "wheel of life." Englishman Eadweard Muybridge (1830–1904), who worked mostly in the United States, invented this innovative machine in 1879, and therefore he is frequently known as the "father of motion pictures" (Figure 2.1). The zoopraxiscope projected a series of images or photographs in successive phases of movement (Solnit 2003:4, 7, 269).

While inventors around the world were developing various aspects of film and motion pictures, in the later part of the 1880s Thomas Edison (1847–1931) and his young assistant, William L. D. Dickson (1860–1935), working in the Edison laboratories in New Jersey, developed a device that recorded visual movement onto celluloid film. In 1891, Dickson created the **kinetograph**, an early motor-powered camera that photographed motion pictures (Library of Congress 2012). In Europe, two Frenchmen, Auguste Lumière (1862–1954) and his

Figure 2.1: In 1878, Eadweard Muybridge, an English photographer, used multiple cameras to visually record "The Horse in Motion." Shot in Palo Alto, California, these twelve images show equine locomotion, and this is one of the earliest examples of motion pictures (*credit: Library of Congress*).

brother Louis Lumière (1864–1948), developed a type of motion picture camera system in 1895, and they began screening their short film productions in Paris cafes (IMDb 2012a, 2012b).

When motion picture development was about three decades old, the earliest documentary was made, the silent film with English **intertitles** called *Nanook of the North*, also known as *Nanook of the North: A Story of Life and Love in the Actual Arctic* (Figure 2.2). Robert J. Flaherty, a Michigan-born writer, **director**, and cinematographer, wrote the documentary. His wife, Frances, purportedly conceived the documentary's topic idea. Because of this documentary and others that Flaherty shot, he is often called "the father of the documentary film" (*Encyclopædia Britannica* 2011). Prior to documentary filmmaking, Flaherty was an explorer and prospector living in Canada, so he knew the people and the region of northern Canada. Shot along Hudson Bay and Ungava Peninsula in the province of Quebec, Canada, *Nanook* is a rather romantic depiction of indigenous people pitted against the harsh environment of the Canadian subarctic region. The film follows an Eskimo (Inuit) named Nanook, his wife, and their children as they hunted, fished, and

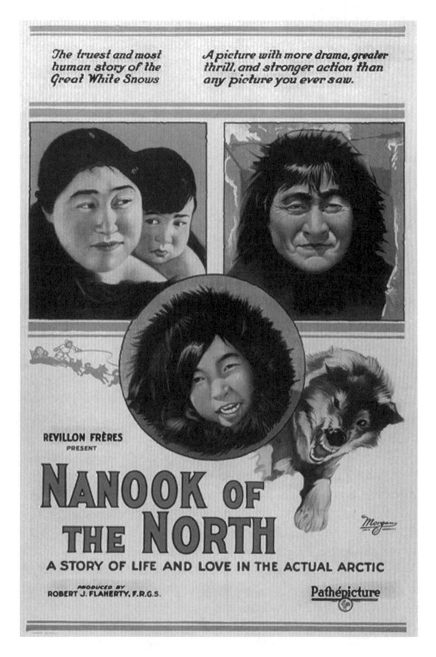

Figure 2.2: *Nanook of the North*, a silent documentary, is the story of an Inuit hunter and his family living in northern Canada. Released in 1922, this documentary by Robert J. Flaherty is considered by most film scholars to be the first documentary film (*credit: Library of Congress*).

traded to subsist in the wilds of the subarctic. The French-funded documentary was released on June 11, 1922, and it was an instant hit. Shot in black-and-white film, the 79-minute-long production reportedly had a working budget of $53,000 (IMDb 2011a).

Over the years, however, this early documentary has received some criticism for not being a true ethnographic record of Inuit society. Flaherty apparently staged some shots. Furthermore, the Inuit who portrayed Nanook, whose real name was Allakariallak, reportedly hunted with a rifle, whereas in the documentary Nanook was portrayed using an Inuit harpoon. Also, to get interior shots inside an igloo, the Inuit documentary and support crew built an open igloo; this not only allowed in ample light but also accommodated the bulky cameras of that era, which were impossible to get inside the small quarters of a regular igloo. Regardless, criticism of Flaherty's work in *Nanook of the North* has been somewhat tempered because he knew his subjects so well, having spent a great deal of time living among them. The production of *Nanook of the North* is an acknowledged cinematic milestone, and it became a model for the times of how to make a documentary. *Nanook* is still shown today in many anthropology and documentary filmmaking classes on American college campuses (IMDb 2011a).

In 1989, the National Film Registry (http://www.loc.gov/film/registry_titles.php), created by the 1988 National Film Preservation Act passed by Congress, listed *Nanook of the North* as one of the first twenty-five films in this prestigious registry as being "culturally, historically, or aesthetically significant." Each year, twenty-five films are added. It is well worth a few minutes of your time to peruse the National Film Registry website to see the list of great movies and documentaries. The National Film Preservation Board and the Librarian of Congress continue their work in seeking public nomination of films for this registry. For a film to be eligible, it must be at least ten years old and be "culturally, historically, or aesthetically significant" (Library of Congress 2011).

Robert J. Flaherty continued his career in documentary filmmaking, producing other well-received documentaries, such as *Moana* (1926), *Tabu* (1931), *Man of Aran* (1934), *The Land* (1942), and *Louisiana Story* (1948). He died in 1951 in Dummerston, Vermont (IMDb 2012c).

While Flaherty was experimenting with documentary filmmaking in the early 1920s, another documentarian was emerging halfway around the world, in the Soviet Union. Sergei Eisenstein (1898–1948) was university-trained as an engineer, and shortly after the fall of the tsar in Russia in 1917, he worked for the Red Army. He soon began to design and build theater sets. He eventually went into filmmaking, and in 1925, Eisenstein released *Battleship Potemkin*, about a 1905 anti-tsarist mutiny aboard a Russian battleship. That mutiny is seen as an event leading up to the Bolshevik Revolution, often called the Red October Revolution, in 1917. Though Eisenstein only made seven films, he is known as the "father of cinematic **montage**" for his frequent utilization of several heavily edited film sequences designed for emotional impact (IMDb 2011b). Another one of Eisenstein's noteworthy documentary films is the 1928 silent film, *October: Ten Days That Shook the World*, about the October 1917 Bolshevik Revolution that put the Communists in control of Russia, thus establishing the Soviet Union (Hampe 2007:14).

Enter Television

Whether documentaries record the present or recall events about people of the past, or feature a combination of past and present, the invention and development of television certainly helped bring documentaries into the public eye. Prior to the popularity of television, documentary films were exclusively viewed in theaters.

Television was created as a result of many inventors from numerous countries working over several decades to use electromechanical methods to scan, transmit, and then reproduce an image. Commercial television has been around since the 1920s, although the medium first dates back to 1884, when German inventor Paul Nipkow (1860–1940) patented the scanning disc, a type of image **rasterizer** (Baird Television 2012a). In the mid-1920s, Scottish inventor John Logie Baird (1888–1946) succeeded in demonstrating televised silhouette images in motion (Baird Television 2012b). During this time, another early experimenter of mechanical television was Charles Francis Jenkins (1867–1934) (Baird Television 2012c). While inventors from around the world were tinkering with this innovation, in 1934 Philo T. Farnsworth (1906–1971), working out of Philadelphia, gave the first public demonstration in America of an all-electronic television system that used a live camera (Massachusetts Institute of Technology 2012). RCA then introduced a functioning television at the 1939 World's Fair in New York City, but World War II temporarily interrupted development of further advances in the technology. Soon after the end of the war in 1945, general television use emerged in the United States and elsewhere. Broadcast television used radio transmissions in **analog** fashion in the frequency band of 54–890 MHz to create sight and sound on television sets (Stephens 2012). You might recall that it was in 2008 when television in the United States shifted from analog to digital format.

As more and more television sets found their way into American households in the 1950s and 1960s, the viewing of documentary programs likewise shifted from theatrical release to documentary television series and programs. One of the most watched archaeological and paleoanthropological documentary-style television programs during this era was the 1966 National Geographic special, *Dr. Leakey and the Dawn of Man* (IMDb 2012d). The program excited television viewers about Louis and Mary Leakey's discovery of *Homo habilis*, an extinct species of humans found in Olduvai (also known as "Oldupai") Gorge in Tanzania, Africa.

3
THE INTRODUCTION OF HOME VIDEO, TELEVISION, AND DOCUMENTARY FILMMAKING

B EFORE EXAMINING THE INTRODUCTION of video to the documentary film-making genre, a brief review of the advent of film, audio, color, and video into filmmaking is necessary.

The Early Years of Movies

By the beginning of the twentieth century, the motion picture industry had matured: filmmakers had learned to dramatize narratives rather than just shoot **scenes,** as had been the norm in the early days of film-making. New York City and New Jersey were early motion picture centers because that is where filmmakers could find actors, props, theatrical experience, and, of course, money to fund movies (Bean 2008:42). Around 1901, Jacksonville, Florida, emerged as a popular location for the silent motion picture industry, as northern filmmakers came south for a longer outdoor filming "season" (Bean 2008:19–49, 62–79). Then, around the time of World War I (1914–1918), Hollywood, California, became the filmmaking center. Not only did southern California have wonderful weather year round, Hollywood and the west coast had a greater variety of outdoor scenery (Dixon and Foster 2008:31). Sound was eventually brought into the silent film experience, too, as motion

Documentary Filmmaking for Archaeologists, by Peter Pepe and Joseph W. Zarzynski, 31–36. © 2012 Left Coast Press, Inc. All rights reserved.

picture theater proprietors hired musicians to play music to accompany silent film screenings. At first this was done to drown out the heavy mechanical noises generated from early cinema projectors. However, soon after the First World War ended in 1918, silent films often came with sheet music, essentially "film scores," for musicians to perform at local theaters during silent film screenings.

Early silent movies had their stars—Charlie Chaplin, Buster Keaton, and Mary Pickford—who were well-known film stars celebrated by Americans and Europeans alike (Dixon and Foster 2008: 35–36). During the decade of the 1920s, however, silent films began to be replaced by productions created with spoken dialogue; these motion pictures soon became known as "**talkies**" or "talking pictures."

Black-and-white films were the mainstay for movies and documentaries until color tinting and finally **Technicolor** production became more prominent. The introduction of full color to Hollywood movies came in the three-strip Technicolor movie *Becky Sharp*, released in 1935. In 1939, possibly Hollywood's greatest year for film production, two mega-movie productions shot in Technicolor—*The Wizard of Oz* and *Gone with the Wind*—were released to large motion picture theater audiences (Dirks 2012). While the big screen was making great leaps in film production, the small screen, television, likewise witnessed technological gains.

The Growth of Television

Although no one person can be credited with inventing television, one of the most significant contributors to television production was a Scottish engineer named John Logie Baird. During the 1920s, Baird and Clarence W. Hansell (1898–1967), an American, used technology based on Paul Gottlieb Nipkow's early television work, and invented a way to transmit images for television. As mentioned in Chapter 2, other innovators at this time, such as Americans Philo T. Farnsworth and Charles Francis Jenkins, were also making significant contributions to the development of early television. Nonetheless, Baird's efforts resulted in a television system of thirty-line images using reflected light rather than just images with back-lit silhouettes. In 1925, Baird's mechanical television system "televised" the first human face, a noteworthy accomplishment (About.com 2012).

A decade and a half later, in 1941, the **FCC** (Federal Communications Commission) issued commercial television licenses to ten American stations, and a few months afterward, WNBT, the first American television station, began commercial broadcasting around the greater New York City metropolitan region. That station eventually changed its call letters to WNBC.

Television grew rapidly in America in the 1950s; and in 1956, the video camera, which was capable of recording both images and sound, was first demonstrated. This groundbreaking piece of equipment sold for $75,000, and CBS television acquired three units that year (ADR Productions 2012).

Home Video Technology

In 1975, Sony introduced **Betamax**, more often called Beta, to the video market. Beta was a consumer-level analog recording technology with a half-inch-wide magnetic videotape in a plastic cassette. This was primarily geared for home video and movie viewing use. The following year, JVC (Victor Company of Japan) released **VHS** (Video Home System). For several years, the Beta and VHS formats battled for control of the home video market. Although Beta was the superior of the two, by the early 1980s VHS finally won the vast majority share of the American consumer market (Vhstodvd.com 2012).

Several VHS-based offshoots soon emerged, such as S-VHS (Super-VHS), with improved picture quality. In 1982, VHS-C (VHS-Compact) was introduced, followed five years later by Super VHS-C (Super VHS-Compact). These smaller videocassettes helped spur the creation of smaller, palm-size **camcorders,** which were played using a **VCR** (videocassette recorder) adapter. There were other varieties of the VHS system, but VHS was soon challenged by 8mm and **Hi8** videocassette systems.

In 1985, Sony released the **Handycam**, a **Video8** camera, and its smaller size quickly overtook the consumer or home camcorder market. This analog system was soon followed by the Hi8 format. Many

professional television and filmmakers welcomed the Hi8 video format because it offered improved picture resolution, and some Hi8 gear
could hold additional digital stereo on a special track. A major problem
for the home video market, however, was that Hi8 videotapes could
not be played on Video8 equipment.

Unfortunately, Beta, VHS, Video8, and their video successors developed image problems from "tape dropout." That is, magnetic particles
from the videotape surfaces simply eroded and literally fell off the tape.
This was especially common on the 8mm format, with its smaller-sized
videotapes and recording heads. Furthermore, the life span of 8mm
videotapes was not very long: tape degradation could start after about
15 years unless the tapes were stored vertically. By the same token, VHS
and Beta tapes used oxide tapes which made them more susceptible to
erasure problems from magnetic fields. (Thus, VHS and Beta videotapes should not be stored near televisions that can create magnetic
fields [Shapiro 2010].) Regardless of the videotape format, all analog
videotapes remaining today should be converted to the digital format
(DVD) for archival purposes to secure the integrity of the image and
audio.

Around the year 2000, the DVD (Digital Versatile Disc) format became the preferred method for distributing Hollywood movies and documentaries. Six years later, in 2006, no new movie titles were being
released in VHS format in the United States.

Of course, by now the digital revolution has fully infiltrated the
professional and amateur filmmaking markets. Initially, film was the
better medium for shooting documentaries because its image quality
was superior to that of video. However, with the introduction of high-
definition video (**HDTV**), documentarians using video could achieve
image quality nearly equal to that of film at a substantially lower cost.
Nonetheless, some documentarians that seek theatrical release for their
documentaries still prefer shooting with film, even as documentaries
shot in HDTV can have terrific image production on the big screen as
well as on television or DVD (Hampe 2007:42).

Earlier in this chapter, we suggested that archaeologists and other
social scientists who undoubtedly have cardboard boxes full of now-
aging videotapes—Beta, VHS, VHS-C, Video8, 8 mm, other analog
video formats—transfer these to DVDs. Analog video can break down,
as it uses an electrical signal stored on magnetic tape. Degradation of

VHS and other analog video can occur in as little as five years. However, the digital video signal utilizes a series of zeroes and ones to produce its video image. Once this is captured, there is no variation in the original signal and an exact copy of the original remains intact, provided it is stored correctly.

Digital video formats include MiniDV, Digital8, MicroMV, DVCam cassette tapes, DVD and mini-DVD, as well as camcorders that use **hard drives** or memory sticks to capture the images and sound. The standard today in documentary filmmaking is to shoot video in HDTV (**16:9 format**). If you are still using an old analog video camcorder, it is time to embrace the digital revolution and go out and purchase an HDTV video camera. Should you succeed in working with professional documentarians on an archaeology-related project, they will certainly appreciate your video camera upgrade.

4
PRODUCTION EQUIPMENT AND SCREEN AND STANDARDS FORMATS

THE DOCUMENTARIAN IN THE archaeologist/documentarian collaboration team will make most of the production's technical decisions. Nevertheless, the archaeologist should have some basic knowledge of video production equipment and the various formats in this medium. With that newfound awareness on the archaeologist's part, the duo will be able to better communicate during the documentary filmmaking process to come up with the best possible product.

The Video Camera

One of the most common questions asked of documentarians by archaeologists is: "What type of video camera should I be using for my work to capture fieldwork and other related video footage?" This chapter answers that and gives more information on the nuances of filmmaking production equipment.

In today's market (2012–2013), there are three types of digital video cameras. Let's start with the basic type and work up. The entry-level unit is the consumer digital video camera. Although digital video cameras were introduced in 1986 with the Sony D-1 format, it was not until many years later that digital video reached the consumer market.

Documentary Filmmaking for Archaeologists, by Peter Pepe and Joseph W. Zarzynski, 37–42. © 2012 Left Coast Press, Inc. All rights reserved.

Today's consumer digital video camcorders are characterized by low price, simplicity of use, and portability. Even many smart phones (such as the newer versions of Apple's iPhones), some digital single lens reflex cameras, and tablet computers such as the iPad have HDTV video camera capability. However, the audio recording capability of these devices is not up to professional standards, as too much **ambient sound** is inadvertently captured. Furthermore, the video camera features on consumer-level units are mostly automatic and therefore are limited in the range of technical options that professional documentarians prefer to use. High-definition digital video consumer camcorders cost only a few hundred dollars, and therefore their low price is attractive to the casual videographer.

Although consumer digital video camcorders today are better, cheaper, and more reliable than in the past, archaeologists might want to invest in the next level of digital video camcorders, more commonly known as **prosumer cameras**. Prosumer digital video cameras generally cost about $1,500 or more and have the look and feel of professional-grade gear without really attaining that level. Many amateur and independent documentarians use prosumer cameras. Most prosumer cameras have relatively high compression ratios, small sensors, and lower optical quality than professional-grade cameras. They have good image quality, with more manual adjustments than consumer-grade camcorders, but generally do not have the ability to utilize interchangeable lenses. Some prosumer cameras have many auto settings, too. For audio, these cameras have an onboard microphone or an input port for hooking up an external microphone. If you are recording interviews, it is an absolute must that your camcorder have the capability of using a wired microphone or a wireless microphone system, as many camera-mounted microphones are not up to professional standards. Most prosumer digital video cameras are quite adequate for shooting archaeological fieldwork to document the stages of your work as long as you shoot in HDTV.

Experienced documentary filmmakers generally use professional-grade HDTV cameras, which cost $5,000 or more. With recent technological advances, the cost of professional video cameras has decreased dramatically, and their portability has increased remarkably as well. These professional cameras give the user greater creative control and fewer auto features. Professional cameras also have larger imaging chips, and they tend to be a bit bulkier than prosumer cameras and are often shoulder-mounted. They also have superior imaging and the capacity to use interchangeable lenses. Because of the preponderance of manual features, professional-grade digital video cameras fare best in the hands of experienced videographers and documentarians.

When purchasing a digital video camera, the videographer must decide whether to get a camera that uses tape or one that has a hard drive. Lighter-weight cameras often use the MiniDV format. These are small 60-minute cassette tapes. It is important to note that when using these tapes, you should always shoot in the SP (standard play) mode and not in the LP (long play) mode that some casual videographers sometimes select. The SP mode delivers better audio and image quality than the LP mode. Some digital video cameras record onto hard disc drives. When the hard drive fills up, you need to download that footage to a computer. One must weigh the pros and cons of tape versus hard drive, or get a camera that permits both.

Regardless of the type of digital video camera you have, you should always shoot your video footage in the high-definition 16:9 aspect ratio format, today's industry norm for documentaries shot in video. Also, you may want to choose the 24 frames per second frame rate rather than 30 frames per second, as the former will produces a film look, which is more appealing to the critical eye.

Sound and Lighting Equipment

Quite often, a documentary film production team will comprise only two field personnel: the documentarian and the archaeologist. Thus, the archaeologist may serve multiple roles, including **P.A. (production assistant** to the director), **gaffer** (lighting technician), and even **boom operator** (microphone assistant who uses a boom pole with attached microphone).

Many inexperienced documentary filmmakers overlook the audio element of production, an oversight easily detected in the muffled sound of poor audio recording. Unfortunately, poor audio is generally difficult to correct in **postproduction,** so if you want to invest in a prosumer camera for documentary footage, make sure it has good microphones. Camera-mounted microphones are satisfactory when shooting secondary footage (known as **B-roll)** to get ambient sound, but not adequate for shooting interviews, which require superb sound quality. For interviews, make sure your camera can use the lapel or **lavalier microphone** that clips to a person's shirt, tie, or jacket. Professional documentary filmmakers will also often use a second kind of external microphone, the directional or boom microphone attached to a boom pole.

If interviews or B-roll are shot inside a building, additional lighting may be necessary to get a quality image. If so, the archaeologist may be called upon to assist in setting up the lighting. The typical setup for an interview might be a two- or three-light configuration. The key light is normally placed in front of the **interviewee**. This light generally has the strongest illumination. A second light may be used as a fill light (to reduce contrast or illuminate something in shadow). Sometimes a third light may be utilized as a back light (high above and behind the subject, to highlight the subject's head from the background). The back light and fill light generally have less illumination than the key light.

Another instrumental piece of equipment in lighting for documentary productions is the **reflector**, generally circular or rectangular in shape, which is used in both well-lit and dark conditions to optimize lighting. Outside in daylight, it can be used to direct sunlight to illuminate areas of light and shadow. At night or inside a building, a reflector might be utilized to create a soft light source.

If you are assisting the director, always wait for instructions on how to carry this equipment, to help set up the gear, and to assist in breaking down this expensive and fragile apparatus. Lights are hot, and with lighting cables on the ground, there is always the chance of tripping and hurting oneself or damaging costly production gear (Lindenmuth 2010:50–53).

Screen Proportions

You may have heard of 4:3 versus 16:9 aspect ratio and wondered what was meant by that. The 4:3 aspect ratio has been in use since the early days of television. Simply stated, this is the image's width-to-height ratio. During the early part of the first decade of the twenty-first century, both television sets and computer screens began to change from a

4:3 to a 16:9 aspect ratio. The newer format, sometimes called "wide-screen," is considerably wider in relation to its height and is being adopted to better accommodate the proportions of movies produced for theater screens

Sometimes when you are watching an older documentary on a wide-screen television, you will see what is called "**pillarboxing**." This is when the program is shown in its original 4:3 aspect ratio format but adds a black bar on the left and right sides to fill up the extra width of the wide-screen TV. Sometimes on an HDTV wide-screen, you will see that an original image has been stretched and distorted to fit the wider space, commonly called "**stretch-o-vision**." Moving in the other direction—watching a program shot in a wide-screen **aspect ratio** on a standard-width TV—you see other ways of making the image fit. One is to zoom in on the image and cut off part of the left and right sides of the image. Another, called "**letterboxing**," maintains the wide-screen aspect ratio but adds a black bar above and one below the image to fill in the extra height. If all this were not confusing enough, other aspect ratios are used in the European motion picture industry, and these may show up on your home screens as well.

Technical Standards for Frame Rate, Resolution, and Color

Have you ever wondered what the abbreviation **NTSC** means on the cover of your favorite DVD or **Blu-ray** case? It stands for National Television System Committee, which is the television system used in the United States, most of the rest of North America, as well as parts of South America, Japan, and parts of Asia and the Pacific region. This is somewhat baffling to the layperson, but this set of standards broadcasts at 60 half-frames per second and 525 lines of resolution. Confusing? Yes. Another system is **PAL** or Phase Alternating Line. This encoding broadcast system is in use in parts of South America, most of Europe, most of Africa, parts of Asia, and in Australia and New Zealand. It utilizes 50 half-frames per second and 625 lines of resolution. Finally, a third major system is in use in some countries. Called **SECAM,** the acronym for the French Système Électronique pour Couleur avec Mémoire (in English, Sequential Color with Memory), this system is found in France, Russia, a few small countries in Europe, many countries that were former French colonies in Africa, parts of Asia, and elsewhere. Over the years, there have been offshoots of SECAM, too.

It is important to note that if you are working in a foreign country and contracting with a local video production service that does not shoot in NTSC, the video must undergo a standards conversion process to be compatible with the format you will be using in postproduction. If you are producing in the NTSC standard and wish to show your documentary in a foreign country that does not utilize this standard, it must likewise undergo a standards conversion in order to be televised. Thankfully, there are many equipment manufacturers that offer tape decks and players that have the ability to output in standards other than the one in which the cassette or file was produced.

5
THE POPULARITY OF DOCUMENTARIES

MANY PEOPLE WITH AN INTEREST in archaeology got their first exposure to the subject by watching a documentary. Whether that initial documentary was shown in school on 16mm film, VHS videotape, DVD, or was broadcast on television, the documentary genre has brought people to places they most likely would never visit to witness incredible archaeological discoveries and investigations. Regardless of where you saw your first archaeology or anthropology documentary, over the decades television has been the main venue for most such productions. Therefore, if you plan to produce an archaeology documentary, a brief history of archaeology documentaries on television and the Internet is a good place to begin.

A Brief History of Television Documentaries

For many people, their first archaeology documentary-style production may have been a National Geographic Society (NGS) creation. NGS, based in Washington, DC, has been around since 1888, providing the viewing public with programs about geography, archaeology, natural science, and environmental and historical conservation issues. After all, NGS's motto has been "inspiring people to care about the planet" (National Geographic 2012). In 2012, this motto was put to the ultimate test, as archaeological professionals were joined by thousands

Documentary Filmmaking for Archaeologists, by Peter Pepe and Joseph W. Zarzynski, 43–50. © 2012 Left Coast Press, Inc. All rights reserved.

of members of the general public in petitioning the National Geographic Channel to pull its new television show *Diggers*, about treasure hunters using metal detectors to find and collect historical artifacts. Following the loud public outcry, the network acted promptly and canceled the show. However, a similar television program called *American Digger*, on Spike (formerly Spike TV), was not canceled, although they received numerous letters, petitions, e-mails, and telephone calls.

In any event, besides publishing its award-winning magazine, NGS documentary-style programs have been on television for decades. Their television series was first aired on CBS (Columbia Broadcasting System) in 1964, before shifting in 1973 to ABC (American Broadcasting Company) and then moving to PBS (Public Broadcasting Service) in 1975. Featured in those NGS programs were scientific luminaries such as Louis and Mary Leakey, Jacques Cousteau, George Bass, and Bob Ballard. In 2001, NGS launched the National Geographic Channel in collaboration with Fox Broadcasting Company.

National Geographic Channel International and History Channel (Canada) broadcast a popular discovery and archaeology-based television series called *The Sea Hunters*. The series (36 espisodes) ran from 2001 to 2006. It was based on a book of that same name by acclaimed novelist and shipwreck discoverer, Clive Cussler. John Davis, based out of Halifax, Nova Scotia, Canada, originally produced the show for Eco-Nova Productions. All episodes included appearances by James P. Delgado, a well-known underwater archaeologist, who served as *The Sea Hunters* program host (Figure 5.1). Clive Cussler likewise was featured in episodes of *The Sea Hunters* (IMDb 2012e). According to Delgado (personal communication, 2012), the television series highlighted some impressive underwater archaeology projects. Among them were shows on Kublai Khan's 1281 invasion fleet of Japan; an underwater search of the World War II V-2 rocket caves in the Harz Mountains in Germany; a survey in the Florida Keys to study the wreck of the *Queen of Nassau*; the eighteenth-century Dutch shipwreck *Vrouw Maria*, lying off Finland, which carried a cargo of valuable art; the 1860s-built undersea vessel the *Sub Marine Explorer*, resting in shallow water off Panama; and fieldwork at the wreck of the *Fox*, an early Arctic exploration ship. Episodes from this series were broadcast in most of the television-viewing countries of the world, making it one of the most widely watched shipwreck discovery and underwater archaeology television series of

Figure 5.1: James P. Delgado, an underwater archaeologist and program host for the popular television series *The Sea Hunters*, communicates with diver Michael Fletcher as the research and television production team documents the wreck of the British warship, the screw steam HMS *Doterel*, which sank off Punta Arenas, Chile, in 1881 (*credit: James P. Delgado*).

the last decade. Some episodes of *The Sea Hunters* television series can be viewed on YouTube, and several are also available to the public as a boxed DVD set.

Possibly your first archaeological documentary viewing was a show on PBS. PBS was founded in 1969 and it started television broadcasting in 1970. *NOVA*, a highly acclaimed PBS series that was first aired in 1974 and was produced by Boston's WGBH, has shown many archaeology-, anthropology-, and history-related television programs (IMDb 2012f). In the first year of *NOVA*, the series broadcast archaeology shows such as *The Mystery of the Anasazi*, about the Ancestral Pueblo peoples of America's Southwest, and *The Men Who Painted the Caves*, a show about the Cro-Magnon people living in France's Dordogne Valley about 15,000 years ago who painted pictures in their cave dwellings (Public Broadcasting Service 2012a). For nearly four decades, the *NOVA* series has informed and delighted many viewers about fascinating archaeological sites and anthropological studies.

One of the most widely viewed archaeology television series in the United Kingdom is *Time Team*. The British series has an interesting concept that is extremely popular with its viewers. A group of archaeologists and other scientific specialists conduct an archaeological dig at a site over a three-day time period as the host explains in layman's terms what is happening. In the United States, a spin-off of this series, entitled *Time Team America*, has been aired on PBS.

Today, in most respects and instances, PBS television documentary-style shows aspire to higher production standards than those in most commercial television programming. For example, if re-creations of actual events are presented, then PBS productions make that fact clear, in order to preclude misleading the viewers in any way. PBS's television production ethics are defined in an eleven-page document published on June 24, 2011, entitled "PBS Editorial Standards and Policies" (Public Broadcasting Service 2012b).

Another eminent television outlet for documentary-style archaeology programs has been The Learning Channel (TLC). Originally created as the Appalachian Community Service Network in 1972 to broadcast educational programming, it was renamed The Learning Channel in 1980 (Education Resources Information Center 1982). In 1991, Discovery Communications, Inc. (DCI), based out of Silver Spring, Maryland, acquired TLC and began broadcasting a popular *Archaeology* series that ran for several years. Produced by Tom Naughton of New Dominion Pictures in Virginia Beach, Virginia, it was based on articles that had been published in *Archaeology* magazine. The TLC series was hosted and narrated by Welsh actor John Rhys-Davies (IMDb 2012g). This series had a local impact upon us, since the production company came to our area, the Glens Falls/Lake George, New York region, and shot a couple of television episodes. One show was about the British and provincial garrison named Fort William Henry (1755–1757), the historic frontier fortress from the French and Indian War that was the setting for James Fenimore Cooper's 1826 novel, *The Last of the Mohicans*; another TLC show was about the colonial soldier Robert Rogers.

One of American television's most popular channels for programming about history and archaeology is called, simply, History (formerly, the History Channel). Created in 1995, it is owned by A&E Television Networks, based in New York City. In addition to the traditional documentary-style programming that has succeeded for them in the past, more recently History has been broadcasting reality-television series such as *American Pickers*, *Ax Men*, *Ice Road Truckers*, *Mudcats*, *Pawn Stars*, and *Swamp People* (History 2012). These shows are not related to history but are outrageous entertainment, and can perhaps even be considered modern-day television versions of the nineteenth-century Western frontier.

A giant in cable television and documentary-type programming is Discovery Communications, Inc. (DCI), which calls itself "The World's #1 Nonfiction Media Company" (Discovery Communications 2012). The company started out as the Discovery Channel back in 1985. Today, DCI includes such cable stations as Discovery Channel, The Learning Channel, Animal Planet, Science Channel, Discovery Kids, Planet Green, Military Channel, Discovery Health, and other popular cable stations. Some of the Discovery Channel's hit shows include *Dirty Jobs* (with popular celebrity host Mike Rowe), *Deadliest Catch*, *MythBusters*, *Planet Earth*, and a popular public favorite, *Shark Week*. Furthermore, the Discovery Channel, in collaboration with the American Film Institute, hosts one of the largest documentary film festivals in the world called **Silverdocs**. This prestigious and well-liked film festival is held each June for one week in Silver Spring, Maryland.

Internet Television and Online Video Sharing

An emerging source for viewing archaeology documentaries and other video programming is Internet TV (ITV or **Internet television**). This is where television shows and other productions, including documentaries, are "delivered" to viewers via the Internet, as people choose what they want to view from an archive or directory. The highly advertised Hulu.com in the United States is an example of this delivery system.

The greatest video phenomenon on the Internet is the video-sharing website YouTube, and many short archaeology videos have been posted there. Three men—Steve Chen, Chad Hurley, and Jawed Karim—founded YouTube in 2005 (under the domain name of "YouTube.com"). In late 2006, Google purchased YouTube for an astonishing price of $1.65 billion (Fast Company 2012). This website and others like it have incredible potential for showing short documentaries to the interested public, but without direct financial remuneration to the documentarian.

YouTube is successful for several reasons. First, the partnership of a highly recognized website—YouTube.com—with Google's powerful search engine is a definite winner. Of course, YouTube has great name recognition. And it has some very user-friendly features, such as showing the number of views, allowing viewers to post comments, offering an easy way to search for and watch videos, and providing a list of videos that are similar to the one you are watching.

Posting a video on YouTube is fairly simple. Although it is not necessary to have a YouTube account, having one makes it much easier to upload and maintain your videos or to delete them if you wish. All you have to do is to open a personal Google account, then simply log in to Google, type in "YouTube" on the search line, and utilize your Google account to set up a YouTube account on that site as well. You can then upload your own videos and give them titles and tags. *Tags* are words that viewers might use to look for specific information in a search engine. For example, if your video is about a French and Indian War shipwreck located in New York state, you might insert tags for your video such as *shipwreck, New York, underwater archaeology*, and *French and Indian War*. There is no limit to the number of tag words you can use to help viewers find your video on YouTube.

Quite often when filmmakers or documentarians have released a new production, they will upload a trailer of their video to YouTube. Web addresses or download sites can be graphically annotated onto the video to help viewers find information about where to purchase the full version or to find out more about the documentary or its **producers**.

Several years ago, The Archaeology Channel (TAC) was formed, an outgrowth of the Archaeological Legacy Institute, a not-for-profit corporation based in Oregon that is primarily supported by memberships and donations. TAC streams archaeology-related documentary videos for public education purposes (The Archaeology Channel 2011).

Finally, many well-financed documentaries seek theatrical release first and then follow with DVD release and/or release using Netflix or similar direct viewing options. These outlets are discussed in greater detail in Chapter 22.

The public's appetite for well-produced and intriguing archaeology documentaries has been a staple for ninety years. With the emergence of numerous cable stations and ITV, and with the expectation of future delivery systems, this demand most certainly will continue to grow. Thus, any archaeologist wishing to create and deliver an enlightening documentary to the public has, and will continue to have, many different options for its release. It is now time to review how to take your **idea** for a documentary and to develop and shape it into a documentary production.

6
THE STAGES OF DOCUMENTARY FILM PRODUCTION

IN THIS CHAPTER, WE LOOK AT THE "big picture" and outline our twelve stages of the documentary filmmaking process, briefly commenting on each. This will give the archaeologist a clearer understanding of how a documentary is put together. The more the archaeologist knows about this process, the better prepared he or she will be to give expert archaeological input into the project. In later chapters, we reexamine some of these points, adding more information (Figure 6.1).

1. Idea or Concept

The idea is the so-called seed, the very beginning. The documentary idea or concept is a generalization, summarized in one or two sentences, and often includes a working title for the documentary and a question (see Chapter 7).

2. Preliminary Research

A superb documentary often stands on a foundation of solid research. The initial research, generally gathered by reading books, reports, newspapers, and Internet-generated articles, is designed to pull together a basic framework on the topic to assist the documentary filmmaking team in crafting the proposal. The proposal for an archaeology- or history-related documentary sometimes includes historical background. Therefore, the archaeologist partner in the documentary collaboration

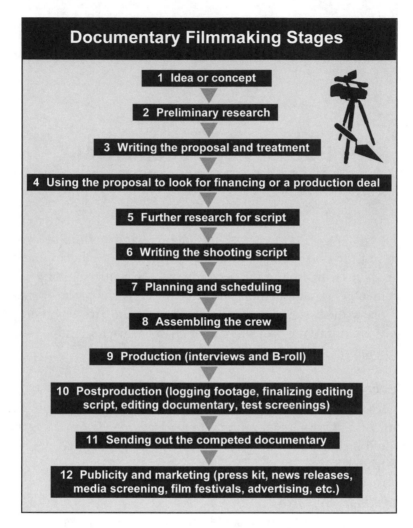

Figure 6.1: Stages of documentary filmmaking.

will play an integral role throughout the documentary process but especially early on in the project, to provide expert advice on research.

3. Writing the Proposal and Treatment

Drafting the two documents, the proposal and the treatment, is a key part of documentary filmmaking, since they lead to the **greenlight** and a contract to produce the documentary. There is no standard format for a proposal, but it is generally three to five pages (double-spaced) or slightly longer, and it includes an estimated budget. The proposal is designed to stimulate interest on the part of the recipient and to get that person to request the treatment (two to twenty pages long, double-spaced). Documentary filmmaker Barry Hampe calls the treatment the "blueprint for a script" (Hampe 2007:193). We explain these items more fully in Chapter 8.

4. Using the Proposal to Seek Financing or a Production Deal

Once the proposal is complete, it is time to use it to pitch your documentary film project. Whether your goal is to sign a deal to make your documentary for broadcast on television, to obtain funding for theatrical release, or simply to have your work shown as part of a museum exhibit, you may need to secure some type of funding. Here you are selling your documentary idea along with the skills and expertise of your archaeology team and the documentary filmmaking crew, too (see Chapter 8).

5. Further Research

Once you close a deal to work on a documentary production, you probably will need to conduct further research, through Internet searches, telephone interviews, and archival work. Fact checking is likewise integral to an accurate archaeology documentary. Therefore, when necessary, bring in expert advisors to complement the team to ensure your documentary is factual (Bernard 2011:119–132). The research phase of your project is also when you begin to hunt down still images and archival stock footage for filming.

6. Writing the Shooting Script

Documentaries can be either scripted or unscripted. Scripted documentaries are the most common and are generally about something that has already happened. To write a script, you must have some definite idea of what happens in the story, who is going to be interviewed, what specific questions are going to be asked of the interviewees, and how the story ends. Unscripted documentaries, by contrast, are usually observational documentaries about events that are currently unfolding. They often have just a list of questions by the interviewer and are less structured. That is, even unscripted documentaries have some degree of scripting, but less than one using a formal **shooting script**.

The shooting script, sometimes referred to as the "shooting treat-ment," is for use by the documentary filmmaking crew. It is often the next progression beyond the original treatment, which was used to help get your funding. Remember, documentary scripts evolve as the docu-mentary filmmaking project moves ahead. The shooting script describes the parts of the documentary that the crew intends to tell. It informs the documentary team which people need to be interviewed, what B-roll has to be shot, and so on. Sometimes the shooting script is nothing more than an outline, essentially a two-column format. Sometimes this outline is written from the initial treatment. It might start out with the "visual" aspect listed on one side of a piece of paper and the "idea line" on the opposite. Or you might have progressed so that you have the "video" on the left side and the "audio" on the right side of your sheet. Regardless, the shooting script is a general plan set forth on paper to aid the production crew. The director, scriptwriter, and archaeologist, in conjunction with other key members of the production team, normally draft the shooting script for the archaeology documentary. See Chap-ter 11 and Appendix 3 for more on this topic.

7. Planning and Scheduling

The logistics of planning and scheduling production fieldwork can be a challenge, just as it is for archaeological fieldwork. Among other things, the production team principals need to scout locations, assem-ble the production crew, line up interviews, acquire all permits and for-mal permissions, make travel arrangements, and develop a production schedule. For an archaeology documentary, this is a collaborative under-taking between the director and the crew's location manager, who will interface with the archaeologist to finalize planning and scheduling. See Chapter 12 for more details on this.

8. Assembling the Crew

The documentary proposal provided information about the key per-sonnel in the production team. Now it is time to complete the roster of the production crew. The bigger your production and the larger the budget, the greater the likelihood that you'll need more people in the crew. In many cases, some crewmembers will be responsible for multi-ple jobs. Here is a list of a documentary filmmaking crew for a major production. Later in the book (see Chapter 12), we will explain the tasks that usually come with these job titles.

- Director
- Executive producer
- Producer
- Scriptwriter
- Production assistant [known as P.A.]
- Production manager/coordinator
- Location scout/manager
- Cameraperson
- Boom operator
- Researcher (in your case, this may include the archaeologist)
- **Narrator**
- Voice talent
- Actors/reenactors
- Makeup artist
- Sound designer
- Special effects supervisor (often does animation and/or computer-generated still images)
- Production sound mixer
- Editor
- Music supervisor
- Title designer

9. Production

If your budget has a couple hundred extra dollars, just prior to production you might want to consider ordering polo shirts and caps emblazoned with the name of the video production company or documentary project. Since many of the crew may be contract employees brought in for the work, this clothing can serve to galvanize team unity. Moreover, the visible name on shirts and caps will help create a buzz about the documentary in the locale where the crew is working, and it also shows a degree of professionalism on the part of the production team. It will be $200–$300 well spent. The adage "dress for success" applies here.

The production stage is the middle part of the documentary film-making process. It is when the director and crew record interviews, acquire B-roll, and shoot reenactments if they are needed (Figure 6.2). During the production stage, the director and scriptwriter will do rewrites of the **script**. It is imperative that the archaeologist has input into the various stages of scriptwriting. Far too many times we have watched documentaries and movies in which the director failed to consult with content experts, thus incorporating erroneous information into the production and thus devaluing the production's authenticity and scope. Audiences want informative and exciting productions, but they seldom tolerate movies or documentaries that they believe are not factual and accurate.

Figure 6.2: Documentarian Peter Pepe (*right*) shoots B-roll video footage at an archaeological excavation. The video footage will be used during the editing process to illustrate what an interviewee or the narrator may be discussing (*credit: Joseph W. Zarzynski*).

10. Postproduction

Postproduction is certainly an exciting time in your documentary film-making project. You have completed shooting B-roll and interviews, and it is time to really start shaping the documentary. This is where your team's principals log (or catalog) footage, approve the **editing script**, and then record the narration. If you are incorporating animation, computer-generated still images, art, or graphics into your production, the director works with those technicians to execute that facet of the project. Your editor then normally lays in the audio script, the interviews, and the narration. Next up is the visual editing, followed by the insertion of background music. Captions and titles are then added. Along the way, the editor, director, and archaeologist will review the initial **rough cut** of the documentary to check for any inaccuracies. One or more external screenings of the rough cut might be held, too. **Sound sweetening** and **video sweetening** are then done to polish the production. Additionally, somewhere during postproduction or even earlier, your director and executive producer or producer meet with graphics experts to design and create the cover art for the documentary poster, DVD disc, and DVD box (Figure 6.3). See Chapter 19 for more details.

11. Sending Out the Completed Documentary

This step happens when the production team has completed the documentary and it is ready for release. How you proceed here depends on whether you have decided on self-distribution, third-party distribution via DVD sales and rentals, downloads, theatrical release, or going directly to a television company for broadcast. Chapter 22 has more details.

12. Publicity and Marketing

Publicity and marketing require a full-fledged campaign of producing a trailer, creating a **press kit**, developing a website, holding a promotional screening of the documentary for members of the media, writing and disseminating news releases, creating Internet publicity, sending out review copies, and, if your documentary was not done for television, submitting it to film festivals to promote your team's creation. See Chapter 23 to read more about this.

Figure 6.3: Eye-catching documentary posters, such as this one for the 2005-released documentary, *The Lost Radeau: North America's Oldest Intact Warship*, help to promote documentary productions (*credit: John Whitesel/Pepe Productions & Bateaux Below, Inc.*).

Now that you have the big picture of the stages of documentary filmmaking, we can examine the genesis for an archaeological documentary and learn how it is shaped.

7

CONSIDERING MAKING
A DOCUMENTARY—
YOUR IDEA AND TITLE

M OST EXPERIENCED ARCHAEOLOGISTS probably have at least once in their professional career imagined being involved in a documentary film on their favorite archaeology project. Although every documentary is unique, they all start with the idea, also frequently called the "concept." Documentary filmmaker and author Barry Hampe, in his book *Making Documentary Films and Videos: A Practical Guide to Planning, Filming, and Editing Documentaries*, claims that you should be able "to state the concept in not more than a hundred words" (Hampe 2007:40). That is great advice, but we go a step further and suggest you should be able to present your documentary film idea in far fewer than a hundred words, probably in a sentence or two—conceptualizing a "hook", which, in the documentary filmmaking industry, is called the **tagline**. After all, Samuel Goldwyn, twentieth-century movie mogul, is reported to once have said: "If you can't write your movie idea on the back of a business card, you ain't got a movie." So, let's be realistic. You really are not ready to begin seriously working toward making a documentary program if you cannot synthesize your documentary project into a first-class working title and a couple of sentences that explain it.

Here is one example of an archaeological discovery and subsequent study that evolved into an idea for a documentary film and ended up as an award-winning documentary. This project was, in fact, the genesis for our archaeologist/documentary filmmaker team, so it is a case study we can readily share with you.

The 32-mile-long Lake George nestled in the Adirondack Mountains of upstate New York was the scene of significant fighting between the French and British, each with their own Native American allies, during the French and Indian War (1755–1763). Nearly two and a half centuries after that conflict began, on June 26, 1990, a small all-volunteer underwater archaeology group led by one of this book's co-authors, Joseph W. Zarzynski, used a Klein 595 side-scan sonar to discover a rare and historic colonial shipwreck lying in 107 feet of water in the "Queen of American Lakes." The 1758 British and provincial (colonial) warship, named *Land Tortoise* because of its seven-sided shape and its upper bulwarks that protected the crew, was the sole survivor of a class of eighteenth-century warships called "radeau." The word "radeau" comes from the French word for "raft," but actually it was a type of floating gun battery. Following the find, Bateaux Below, the group that found the shipwreck, produced an archaeological map of this remarkably preserved vessel under the direction of Rhode Island nautical archaeologist Kathy Abbass and Zarzynski. In the early 1990s, Bateaux Below's Zarzynski and his colleague Bob Benway approached corporate and documentary video filmmaker Peter Pepe of Glens Falls, New York, to produce a documentary on the historic warship. Bateaux Below's historian, Russell P. Bellico, had dubbed the one-of-a-kind, 52 × 18 foot wide shipwreck as "North America's oldest intact warship," not only because of the wooden vessel's age but also because of its remarkable structural integrity. Using Bellico's brief description for the 1758 *Land Tortoise* radeau shipwreck, Zarzynski wrote up an idea for the documentary proposal that is summed up in this descriptive sentence, essentially a tagline, for production project:

> This is the story of the history, discovery, and archaeological study of a rare French and Indian War shipwreck nicknamed "North America's oldest intact warship."

Not only was this concise statement the idea for the documentary proposal, Bellico's creative slogan, "North America's oldest intact warship," became the branding phrase for the sunken colonial vessel.

The research team followed up the documentary idea with a multiple-page outline for the documentary, and Zarzynski presented it to

Peter Pepe, owner and director of Pepe Productions, an established local video production corporation whose studio was only a few miles from Lake George. Pepe really liked the documentary idea, but his years of experience told him the timing was just not right to produce a feature-length documentary film on this subject. After all, Bateaux Below was early into the archaeological investigation phase of the research project, and they were just beginning to get an accurate assessment of the sunken vessel's class, how it was built, its function, and what to do to best preserve this iconic British shipwreck. However, nearly a decade and a half later, in 2004, Pepe was again presented with the same documentary idea by local computer animator John Whitesel. Remembering the early 1990s proposal by Bateaux Below, Pepe knew the timing was then just right and that the story had matured into an exceptional and compelling tale that was worth telling. So, Bateaux Below, Pepe Productions, Whitesel Graphics, and Black Laser Learning (a small company that produced training videos on topics related to sonar) collaborated on the documentary project. Eighteen months later, a 57-minute-long documentary on the 1758 *Land Tortoise* shipwreck was finished. Entitled *The Lost Radeau: North America's Oldest Intact Warship*, the documentary eventually won several awards for video production excellence and was shown on PBS television stations around New York state. As an added benefit, it became the genesis for other underwater archaeology documentaries by Pepe Productions. The point of this example to the archaeologist wishing similar success is this: it all started with an idea or concept, the proverbial seed for any outstanding documentary film!

So, once you have your documentary idea and have encapsulated it into a couple of descriptive sentences, take that idea and create an attention-grabbing title. The title may very well change during the many stages of the documentary production—in fact, it often does. However, having a catchy working title early on helps not only to draw people's attention, it also "sells" the project. A memorable title alone can get your feet past the door into the office of a documentary production company. In our view, shorter titles are usually better, as the public will remember them more readily. But whether short or somewhat long, the title is how your project is going to be identified. Therefore, it had better be unique to distinguish your documentary from the many other projects floating around out there.

Here are two other archaeology-related examples of ideas that became award-winning documentaries produced by Pepe Productions and colleagues:

Documentary Title: *Wooden Bones: The Sunken Fleet of 1758* (Pepe Productions in collaboration with Bateaux Below, Inc., 2010, 58 minutes)

Idea or Tagline: This is the story about the history and archaeological investigation of Lake George, New York's "Sunken Fleet of 1758."

And,

Documentary Title: *Search for the* Jefferson Davis: *Trader, Slaver, Raide*r (Pepe Productions in collaboration with the Lighthouse Archaeological Maritime Program, 2011, 50 minutes)

Idea or Tagline: This is the story of the history and archaeological pursuit of a lost shipwreck off St. Augustine, Florida, a Confederate privateer that formerly was a commercial vessel and then illegal slaver before becoming the last great maritime mystery of America's Civil War.

As an exercise to help you select your documentary's working title, take a sheet of paper and draw two vertical lines down the page to create three columns. In the left column, list several titles for your documentary project. In the middle column, write down the pros for each title, and in the right-hand column, state the cons for each title you have listed. Share these with a few close friends and colleagues and ask their opinions. Before you commit to any title, do a web search to make sure your favorite title is not already being used in another project.

Besides having an idea or concept for your documentary, you must also have a really first-rate story to tell. Documentarians first and foremost are storytellers. At Pepe Productions, we have a mantra to describe our documentary filmmaking:

A documentary is a story that has found its storyteller.

Your documentary idea must be an incredible tale just waiting to be told.

Later in the book (Chapter 11), we will guide you through the process of developing your idea and story into a documentary, using a script format. After all, it is estimated that about 80 percent of all documentary productions are scripted (Rosenthal 2007:15). In most cases, then, documentary filmmaking requires creative writing skills to shape the story into a well-crafted script. The storyline must be well thought out, fully researched, and, over time, molded into a script by the filmmaking team. One of the hallmarks of a documentary film is that it is grounded in fact, unlike the creation of a novel, which is fictional.

Now you know the value of crystallizing your idea or concept and the importance of developing a solid working title for your documentary project. Next it is time to learn about pitching your documentary proposal. Chapter 8 takes you through the steps of this make-or-break phase of documentary filmmaking.

8
PITCHING A PROPOSAL AND WRITING A TREATMENT

Preparing the Proposal

WHETHER THE ARCHAEOLOGIST APPROACHES a documentarian to work on a collaborative documentary film project or directly seeks out a television outlet to develop a documentary-style program, a formal proposal will have to be written. In many respects, the proposal is the single most important aspect of the documentary filmmaking journey. There is no standard format for constructing a proposal, unless the television company or funding agency you are approaching has proposal guidelines. Moreover, there is a huge difference between your documentary idea, which is a rather simplistic piece of writing, and a formal proposal, which must be succinct and interesting enough to win over your recipient.

Your documentary proposal should be relatively brief, a few pages long (generally double-spaced). Its sole purpose is to sell your project to the recipient, whether a television commissioning editor, a curious colleague, or others. A successful documentary proposal shows that your team has a solid production idea, that you thoroughly know your topic, that you are professional, and that you should be given a contract (Rosenthal 2007:34). At the very least, the proposal's reviewer should be intrigued enough to reply back and ask for more information. If you are fortunate enough to be invited to provide more information on

Documentary Filmmaking for Archaeologists, by Peter Pepe and Joseph W. Zarzynski, 65–72. © 2012 Left Coast Press, Inc. All rights reserved.

your proposed documentary, you then send in your treatment, often described as the "blueprint for a script" (Hampe 2007:193). This chapter offers insight into developing and pitching a proposal and also writing the all-important document known as the "treatment."

Reviewers seldom have the time to read dozens of pages of a formal documentary proposal. Therefore, a concise proposal document is the suggested norm, although some documentarians actually write several proposals for the same project, each of a different length to fit different recipients. A standard proposal of three to five pages or fewer will test your creative writing skills. Though there is no formal outline for this type of proposal, the items listed in the Sample Documentary Proposal Outline (below) are standard elements.

Sample Documentary Proposal Outline

1. Documentary title and name of production team

2. Documentary statement (short synopsis)

3. Background on the documentary's topic and the need for the production

4. Approach and style

5. Audience

6. Budget

7. Schedule

8. Key production team members, with brief "bios"

9. Miscellaneous

10. Contact information

Now, we examine each of these elements.

1. Documentary Title and Name of Production Team

Centered at the top of your page, write "Documentary Proposal." Skip a line and then give the title of your documentary. On the following line, write the name of the production company or the name of the leading production company, if it is a collaborative endeavor. You can front-load the proposal by inserting some contact information for the production company, but normally the contact information goes at the end of the proposal. Here is an example of a documentary film title and the production company:

Documentary Proposal
Wooden Bones: The Sunken Fleet of 1758
By Pepe Productions

[Note: You can front-load the proposal if you want by including the production company's contact information or wait to do that at the end of the proposal.]

Then in your proposal, briefly address the following.

2. Documentary Statement

The documentary film statement is a brief summary, a paragraph in length, of what the documentary is about. It should state the proposed length of your documentary (in number of minutes), briefly describe the target audience(s), and provide a production timeline. Since this is the first substantive thing the recipient will read about your project, it needs to be a masterful synopsis. Sometimes the success of this paragraph will dictate whether the reviewer will read further. So your documentary film statement needs to be very good.

3. Background on the Documentary's Topic and the Need for the Production

This section gives background on the topic of the documentary and also states why your documentary is needed. Here you explain the ways in which the documentary will be both informative and entertaining, and why it is a "must" production to be made. Let the proposal reader know that your program is unique, containing new information on the subject. Also, explain why the documentary is timely. Use dynamic language, and provide just enough background so that the reader becomes engaged in your project and comes away being supportive, wanting to work with you on producing your documentary.

4. Approach and Style

This section briefly explains how the documentary team plans to approach the program. Any documentary is about a subject from the past, present, or a combination of the two. If it is about the past, can you obtain enough images that the documentary is not limited to video of "talking heads"? What is the documentary's progression? Will you tell the story using a chronological progression? Or will the documentary describe a conflict and seek a resolution? A popular type of progression for archaeology-related documentaries is the search to solve a mystery (Rosenthal 2007: 97–98). Or, is it a hybrid of these progressions? Make sure yous do a good job briefly and clearly explaining how you intend to convey your story.

5. Audience

Your proposal briefly mentioned the audience in the documentary film statement (item 2, page 67), but now you must expand on this to specifically identify and describe the intended audience. Are you making your documentary for a general audience, such as television for viewers of all ages, different educational backgrounds, and varied religious beliefs? Or is your audience a targeted group? Explain how you can attract an audience for your documentary. If you are proposing a series, make sure you delineate how you plan to draw people back to watch the follow-up programs in the series.

6. Budget

The budget need not be detailed but should provide estimates for the various categories of expected costs. You will have to factor in general, **preproduction**, production, and postproduction costs as well as (possibly) distribution expenses. The budget is usually prepared by the documentary filmmaker, who will have the experience to pull this data together. The archaeologist's role will be to guide the documentarian by providing information on the costs associated with research, travel, field and lab expenses, wages, and the like. Fortunately, most archaeologists write grant proposals to support their work and therefore are quite familiar with the all-important budget.

7. Schedule

This section of the proposal provides a brief outline of the timetable for the preproduction, production, and postproduction schedules, indicating the approximate number of weeks or months needed for each. Remember, "Mr. Murphy and his crew of malcontents" are always lurking about any project, ready to cause some type of havoc. Therefore, a little extra time should be built into the overall schedule for such hazards as inclement weather, travel delays, equipment malfunctions, crew illness, editing delays, and the like. It will be essential for the archaeologist to weigh in on the logistics and time-related nuances of archaeological fieldwork and laboratory schedules. Likewise, to ensure that documentary content is accurate and fashioned with archaeological proprieties firmly in mind, the archaeologist should insist on being involved in some capacity in script approval and postproduction documentary review (the time for which should be included in the schedule). If not, you might have a final product that will have archaeological inaccuracies or philosophical differences.

8. Key Production Team Members, With Brief "Bios"

The recipient of your documentary proposal will want to know something about the principals of the filmmaking team. To that end, your proposal should provide a brief biographical sketch ("bio") of each principal, substantiating his or her talent and experience. If your documentary filmmaker has won noteworthy awards, then announce them. The same holds true for the archaeologist. If the archaeologist is a renowned and recognized expert in the field that the documentary will address, then highlight that. If you have access to a VIP to be interviewed, then also put that into your proposal. Celebrities can sometimes "make" your documentary proposal. This is not the time to be humble about your team and those people who have agreed to be interviewed.

9. Miscellaneous

In this section of the proposal, feel free to provide any other information that will help sell your proposal. Nowadays, some filmmaking teams offer to provide a short (two- to five-minute-long) video "teaser." This requires extra work up front for the production crew, but it is a great way to give visual and audio information about the subject of the documentary and to showcase the professional talents of the documentary filmmaking team. If you do not have a teaser for your proposal, be bold: send along a DVD that shows the best documentary work your production team has done in the past. Make sure the DVD is in a case with an attractive cover and that the DVD disc is likewise "dressed for success."

10. Contact Information

At the end of the proposal document, provide contact information for the principal in the documentary filmmaking team. This should include the formal name of the contact, that person's title, the company name, mailing address, e-mail, and the office and cell telephone numbers.

Finally, your proposal package should include a well-crafted single-page cover letter written on business stationery. This will be the first item in your proposal packet that the recipient will see and read, so draft a creative cover letter to introduce yourselves and your project, and pave the way for the recipient to want to read your formal proposal.

To see a sample of one of our documentary proposals, go to Appendix 1 of this book, which presents our proposal for the 2011 documentary *Search for the* Jefferson Davis: *Trader, Slaver, Raider*.

Writing the Treatment

Many novices who venture into the field of documentary filmmaking (and even some fairly experienced documentarians) may be befuddled by the task of writing the documentary treatment. They really do not fully understand it. That may be because documentary films are essentially visual productions and the treatment is a written description of what will be seen and discussed. The treatment, as noted earlier, is the "blueprint" for the documentary, and it is typically written in the present tense as a narrative. The treatment is usually separate from the proposal. Your proposal is intended to introduce your planned documentary and get television companies, production teams, or funding agencies to ask for more.

That "more" is the treatment. In many respects, the treatment is an outline for the script, and thus it explains what the documentary is about, what will be included in the production, and how it will look (Hampe 2007:193–194). The documentary director usually writes the treatment with input from other principals of the project.

As an example, here is the beginning paragraph of a treatment for our award-winning 2005 documentary, *The Lost Radeau: North America's Oldest Intact Warship*. The underlined words indicate what will be seen and heard during the documentary:

> The documentary program begins with <u>B-roll</u> of underwater archaeologists aboard a research vessel on Lake George, New York, conducting a side-scan sonar survey. <u>Narration</u> explains that these researchers, members of Bateaux Below, are using state-of-the-art remote sensing equipment in search of the past, scanning the lake looking for historic shipwrecks from the French and Indian War (1755–1763).

In these first two sentences of the treatment, we have introduced our documentary and likewise have brought the viewers along, making them armchair explorers, "pulling" them into the program. The treatment cites no camera angles and gives no technical jargon. Its goal is to make the production intriguing and to describe what the documentary will show and tell. Because the treatment gives a visualization of what will be in the documentary, this document is normally longer than a proposal. A treatment for an hour-long documentary might be a few pages or even as many as twenty-five pages. In the treatment, you will introduce the people, places, and events that will be featured as well as their order of appearance. You can generalize at times, but where you have strengths—such as a VIP character—be sure to include how you intend to put that advantage to use.

While your treatment must tell a compelling story, you know full well that during production—when you get into the actual interviews, B-roll, and other aspects—your storyline will most likely change, generally for the better. Drafting the treatment is more the creative product of the documentarian, but the archaeologist in the collaboration should have a say in how this is constructed. The more the archaeologist knows about this process, the greater the chance that the he or she will be able to offer constructive input.

Your documentarian colleague will know how to write a treatment, and there are certainly enough books on the market, should you desire to study this topic further (see, for example, Sheila Curran Bernard's *Documentary Storytelling: Creative Fiction on Screen*; Barry Hampe's *Making Documentary Films and Videos: A Practical Guide to Planning, Filming, and Editing Documentaries*; and Alan Rosenthal's *Writing, Directing, and Producing Documentary Films and Videos*). For a synopsis, see our "Points to Consider" below.

Points to Consider When Writing a Treatment

Here are some tips your team should consider when writing a treatment (Atchity and Wong 2003:9–12):

1. Be brief, if possible.

2. Use paragraph form.

3. Use the present tense.

4. Introduce the main people in the documentary.

5. Give the highlights of the documentary without going into too much detail.

6. Use unpretentious language.

7. Describe your hook to grab the viewers.

8. If possible, characterize the conflict in the story.

9. Whenever possible, include the turning points or twists in the story.

10. Be dramatic, not dull, in the telling.

In Appendix 2, we provide a sample treatment for our documentary *Search for the* Jefferson Davis: *Trader, Slaver, Raider*. Remember, there is no set template for a treatment. The treatment style we present in Appendix 2 is one that we felt was most applicable for that documentary.

9
DEVELOPING A BUDGET AND SECURING A CONTRACT

IN CHAPTER 8, WE BRIEFLY TOUCHED ON SOME basic thoughts about your documentary film budget. In this chapter, we expand on that to give you more insight into the money side of documentary filmmaking, and then we examine the process of securing a contract to make a documentary.

Developing a Budget

There are a few things to think about as your documentary filmmaking team frames its budget. For instance, if you are the archaeologist and your goal is to create a quality documentary about your archaeology project that ends up in theatrical or television release, you may not expect to get paid. Nonetheless, there may be direct expenses that have to be covered, such as equipment costs, key team personnel salaries, research costs, and travel expenses. And perhaps you may want to get paid for some of your professional services. Or possibly you are simply developing a budget for your organization to finance a short documentary on one of your projects. Regardless, a formal budget must be devised, and you may be brought into the budget drafting process, so here is a primer.

The following is a simplified budget outline that you can use as a checklist to talk over with your documentary filmmaker.

- General Expenses: Salaries, General Overhead (office rental, telephone, office supplies), Contracts (legal fees), Licenses and Permits, Insurance, Accounting, Photocopying, Shipping, Contingencies, Other

- Preproduction Costs: Research, Travel and Hotel, Proposal and Treatment Writing, Script Writing, Production Planning and Scheduling, Other

- Production Costs: Producer, Director, P.A., Other Crew, **Talent**, Travel and Hotel, Expendables, Videotapes, Camera and Gear (tripod, **jib crane**, reflector, etc.), Audio Equipment, Location Costs, Supplies (videotapes, batteries, replacement pieces, etc.), Meals, Other

- Postproduction Costs: Editing Software, Computer, Narration, Stock Footage and Still Images, Editing, Graphics, Animation (if required), Music, "Sound Sweetening" (audio), "Video Sweetening," Other

- Costs after Documentary is Completed: Design and Printing (documentary DVD disc, DVD box, and DVD poster), Trailer Development, DVD **Replication**, Review and Comp Copy Packaging and Shipping, Film Festival Entry Fees and Associated Travel, Design and Create Website and Other **Social Media**, Traditional Publicity (space ads, postcards, etc.), Miscellaneous Mailing and Shipping, Other

Budget Total

As you work with the documentarian to finalize your budget, be aware that the filmmaking industry normally calculates in "per diem" increments rather than in weekly or monthly increments. However, the director, editor, and production assistants (P.A.s) are normally budgeted per week rather than per diem. Also, even if the documentary filmmaker owns much of the production equipment, there are still budgeting costs attributable to using this expensive gear (Hampe 2007:382–389; Lindenmuth 2010:62; Rosenthal 2007:129–132). Appendix 4 shows a simplified budget that we used for a television program we proposed for a major television channel. Many budgets are simplified like this, but some television channel commissioning agents want to see a more item-ized budget.

Securing a Contract

Obviously, a contract is needed between the documentary filmmaking team and the sponsor, whether the latter is a museum, a television company, a financial backer, a university, or your archaeology group. Legal experts will have to draft or review this. Such contracts might include:

■ Documentary length and purpose: State the length of the documentary in minutes and declare what the documentary will be about.

■ Documentary due date and manner of delivery: This establishes the contracted due date for the documentary and the medium of delivery, such as DVD or BetaSP cassette. If you are doing a short documentary for sale in a museum or historical society gift shop, this section should also state the number of copies that will be provided.

■ Fee owed filmmaking team, including payment schedule: This section clearly states how much will be paid to the production team and specifies the payment schedule.

■ Product approvals: It is important to designate who will be the contact with the sponsor and who will be responsible for reviewing and approving the documentary at the various stages of production. Otherwise, it becomes work by committee, which can jeopardize your ability to meet the final copy due date.

■ Insurance: You might want to include insurance, such as general insurance and errors and omissions (E & O) insurance. The latter is a type of liability insurance that protects individuals and companies against claims of idea theft, defamation, copyright infringement, negligent actions, and other false claims (Wong 2012:37).

■ Ownership: This is important. The documentary filmmaking team will try to retain ownership of the production or at least share in ownership. Ancillary rights should be outlined here, too (Rosenthal 2007:141–145).

Sample contracts are available online from a variety of groups; see the websites of organizations like the International Documentary Association, Writers Guild of America, and others. Since contractual situations often vary, we cannot overstate the importance of consulting with a lawyer who is versed in entertainment law.

10
SHAPING YOUR ARCHAEOLOGICAL DOCUMENTARY

LIKE ANY GOOD PIECE OF ROCK MUSIC, a documentary needs a great beat. This beat comes from the shaping and weaving of your story. Most likely, you already have a subject, an idea, and even a title for your documentary. Now you need to decide what documentary type best fits the way you envision the shape of the documentary. Kevin J. Lindenmuth, in his book *The Documentary Moviemaking Course: The Starter Guide to Documentary Filmmaking*, discusses the four main documentary types: expository, observational, participatory, and dramatic (Lindenmuth 2010: 10–13):

- Expository type: This type tries to persuade the viewer into taking a certain perspective or viewpoint. With this type, there is a heavy emphasis on verbal commentary.

- Observational type: In this type, the filmmaker intervenes very little, as the documentarian serves mainly as an observer with a camera. This type is most appropriate for ethnographic documentaries.

- Participatory type: In this type, the filmmaker is involved as an active participant in the documentary. One of the best examples of this is Morgan Spurlock's 2004 documentary hit, *Super Size Me*, about a man who investigates fast-food addiction and, in so doing, gains over twenty pounds on that kind of diet.

- Dramatic type: This type is quite popular for investigating and telling historical or archaeological events. The story is often told

Documentary Filmmaking for Archaeologists, by Peter Pepe and Joseph W. Zarzynski, 77–82. © 2012 Left Coast Press, Inc. All rights reserved.

using archival film footage, illustrations, interviews, animation, and reenactments.

Another important aspect of shaping and fashioning a documentary is structure—that is, the progression of visuals and audio as they are formulated to grab the audience's attention, present the story's perspective, and culminate in a suitable ending. The age-old formula for relating a story is the three-act play—the setup, confrontation, and resolution. The first act represents about one-quarter of the story's length, the second act is about half of the production, and the third and final act takes up approximately the last quarter of the show. Documentarian Barry Hampe simplifies this structure as "B-M-E," which stands for "beginning-middle-end" (Hampe 2007:173). You may recall this structure from your high school English class, when you learned about story development in creative writing and were told that the three-act play or story format originated with Aristotle from ancient Greece. This formula for storytelling is fashionable even today because most of us enjoy tales with a **closed ending**, that is, where all the details are wrapped up to end the conflict.

As you help the scriptwriter develop the various versions of the script, bring to mind one of your friends, someone who is rather popular in your circle of pals because he or she tells wonderful tales, a born storyteller. Your friend's anecdotes start with a captivating beginning; as you listen, you can literally visualize the location, mood, and theme. The raconteur now has the audience mesmerized and keeps their interest by developing the conflict and possibly even inserting some controversy. Finally, your storytelling buddy leads listeners down the road to the end of the cliffhanger—resolution and closing. That is what a satisfying documentary script does, too. It tells a terrific and enthralling story.

The most popular formats for relating a documentary story are listed in the sidebar and are discussed below.

1. Chronological Story

The chronological format is an ageless style for archaeology or history documentaries. Ken Burns's 1990 PBS documentary, *The Civil War*, is a well-known example of a television production done in this tried-and-true story format. The audience is very familiar with this structure, with its standard beginning, middle, and end. After all, real life is generally like this! That said, even when you use the chronological story format,

Popular Archaeology Documentary Storytelling Formats

1. Chronological Story

2. Crisis, Conflict, and Resolution

3. The Search

4. Hybrid of Story Types

you need not relate events in chronological order. You can start in the middle, go back to the very beginning, and work toward to the end. You've surely seen plenty of documentaries and movies set up using that progression. Likewise, you can use periodic flashbacks, too, so long as you do not change the facts and you end up conveying the story with its chronological record intact.

With all the formats, but especially with this one, less is generally better. No documentary communicates everything. In a documentary that covers a long historical time frame, there is sometimes a desire to give far too many details, dates, and information. It is usually best to relate only the relevant information and let the viewers come to their own conclusions.

2. Crisis, Conflict, and Resolution

Another progression format for documentaries is "crisis, conflict, and resolution," sometimes referred to as the "conflict documentary." Here the crisis and conflict are established early in the story, and the main part of the production is a progression toward final resolution. Viewers should be touched and emotionally connected to the crisis and conflict, drawn more and more into the story until the crisis is finally resolved.

An example of a documentary-style television production that follows the "crisis, conflict, and resolution" story formula is a 2008 National Geographic Channel program entitled *Shipwreck! Captain Kidd*. This engrossing television show follows a team of underwater archaeologists from Indiana University and the Dominican Republic, led by Charles Beeker (Indiana University), as they investigate a late seventeenth-century shipwreck off the Dominican Republic which they believe is one of the vessels captained by the infamous pirate William Kidd. While the story of Captain Kidd, his life, and controversial conviction for piracy is being told, a parallel subplot of great tension emerges. Underwater archaeologists have located one of Captain Kidd's shipwrecks, and there is a race to excavate, raise, and safely transport one of the sunken vessel's cannons to a nearby museum as a Caribbean storm threatens the project. The production successfully examines several storylines: Was Captain Kidd really a ferocious pirate or was he simply a misunderstood privateer? What should be done with this historic shipwreck, the *Quedagh Merchant*, to best safeguard it and also share it with the public? And finally, can the underwater archaeologists raise and then take to port one of the sunken ship's historic cannons as an oncoming gale challenges their efforts?

3. The Search

Back in the mid-1970s and into the decade of the 1980s, one of the most popular documentary-style television series was *In Search of...* The series attracted a wide range of viewers, young and old, interested in mysteries like UFOs, Bigfoot, the Loch Ness monster, missing persons, the lost Roanoke Colony, and other unexplained phenomena. The weekly television series ran from 1976 to 1982. Regardless of the disputed content of some shows, this series probably did more to attract armchair explorers and universalize the search motif for the documentary genre than any previous television program. When Discovery Channel was launched in 1985, it refined the search motif and brought more scientific credibility to this documentary-style genre. Programs like PBS's *NOVA* series and National Geographic films and television shows have harnessed and honed the search motif, now a trendy format, especially for archaeology-related television productions.

4. Hybrid of Story Types

Finally, some documentaries use a hybrid form of these various story progressions. The 1999 PBS *NOVA* series television program *Voyage of Doom* is an example of such a hybrid. The documentary-style program is about Robert Cavelier de La Salle, a seventeenth-century explorer, and his doomed French colony along the shores of Matagorda Bay, Texas. The show focuses around one of his vessels, the *La Belle*, which was sunk in the bay. The program follows the history of the ill-fated colony, the modern-day discovery of the shipwreck, the challenge to excavate the sailing vessel using a cofferdam built around the shallow-water wreck, and the search by archaeologists to uncover previously unknown details about LaSalle's failed colonization attempt.

It is up to your team to decide how to develop your documentary tale. Regardless of how the crew and its scriptwriter fashion and structure your documentary, do not overload it with too much detail. If you have a great storyline and loads of information that cannot be whittled down, you might want to consider developing a mini-series.

Ethics in Documentary Filmmaking

Ethics in documentary filmmaking is a hallmark of the genre, so we remind you that bending or stretching the truth and using poor ethical standards are not the way to produce an archaeology documentary. This is as appropriate a time as any for a few important words on a cardinal rule in documentary filmmaking: adhere to ethics throughout the production process. Colleges and universities have courses devoted to this subject, and many books contain sections on ethics in documentary filmmaking. One book we recommend that has much good material on ethics is *Making Documentary Films and Videos: A Practical Guide to Planning, Filming, and Editing Documentaries* by Barry Hampe. There are also numerous articles and book chapters, too; you may wish to consult, for example, "Ethics" by Kees Bakker in the book *The Documentary Film Makers Handbook*, by Genevieve Jolliffe and Andrew Zinnes (2006). Of course, archaeologists constantly preach ethics in all archaeological endeavors. That holds true in documentary filmmaking, too.

The filter of ethics should suffuse the production process from the very start of your project, through the various scriptwriting versions, into the production and editing stages, and in the final production. You certainly can have opinions and a distinct slant in your documentary, but these should be balanced so your project is not completely one-sided.

Look over our ethics checklist (following). Of course, this is necessarily oversimplified; life as we live it is rarely so clear-cut. If you are in doubt about ethical standards, consult with one or more of your trusted colleagues. Talk it over, and review the literature on the subject.

A Checklist on Ethics in Documentary Filmmaking

Here is a rudimentary checklist of things to consider on ethics in documentary filmmaking (Nichols 2006):

1. Always seek and state the truth in your documentary.

2. Be sincere.

3. Do solid research on your documentary subject so you are, at the very least, a mini-expert, thus minimizing the chances of making factual errors and ethical mistakes.

4. Do not manipulate images or edit interviewee statements to be misleading.

5. If using reenactments, either identify that fact or present the reenactments in a way to ensure it is obvious that the scene is a reenactment.

6. Do not alter the archaeological record (image) by distorting it to fit the screen.

7. Select people who have integrity to interview.

8. Be constantly aware of misrepresentation.

9. Do not use misleading video footage or images.

10. Always get formal permission to use others' images.

11. Obtain a permission release from every person who appears in your documentary.

12. Fact check.

13. Be sensitive to the cultural mores of groups that appear or are mentioned in your documentary.

14. Respect the humanity of your subject.

It is now time to investigate how to move from your idea, your documentary proposal, and your treatment, to developing your outline and then into the various script versions. The archaeologist will assuredly be a principal component in script development, so you need to know about the nuances of documentary scriptwriting.

11
FROM OUTLINE TO
FIRST SCRIPT

SCRIPTS ARE THE BACKBONE of the Hollywood motion picture industry. While not all documentaries are scripted (see Chapter 6), generally speaking, scripts are preferred. As we noted in Chapter 7, scripted productions account for an estimated 80 percent of all documentaries (Rosenthal 2007:15). Scripts play a critical role, functioning like the architect's plan used by contractors when constructing a building.

Documentary scripts almost always evolve over the various stages of production. The process necessarily starts with your idea, then often moves to some type of an outline, then possibly into a treatment, then to a shooting script, and finally to the editing script (Bernard 2011:155). In this chapter, we trace the course of development from an outline to the first script, often the shooting script. It is important to understand up front that your script will almost certainly change and evolve as you record the interviews, make new discoveries during the shooting of B-roll, and finally during the editing process. Keep your mind open to interesting story developments and be flexible enough to seize opportunities if the story seems to diverge from your initial idea, even if it means tweaking or even drastically revising your script.

As a rule of thumb, documentaries that deal with past events are likely to be scripted, whereas documentaries about a current event are often unscripted, as the story's trajectory is largely unknown beforehand. Unscripted documentaries will use some type of an outline, are more spontaneous, often require more production work, and generally require more time for selecting footage during editing (Lindenmuth 2010:28–29).

Before we get into the heart of this chapter, it is imperative to realize that a documentary script is dialogue, whether in the interviews or in finely honed narration. Scriptwriting is thus very different from writing an archaeology report or a professional paper for publication in an archaeology journal. Because the script will be spoken, it is important that the scriptwriter—be it the director, a dedicated writer, or you—read the script out loud to make sure it sounds natural. Find a colleague, friend, or family member who will listen to the script being read out loud when it is still in development. They can be excellent sounding boards, will often provide invaluable and critical feedback, and can definitely aid in polishing the script.

You already have your idea and have developed the proposal, too. You probably have even written some type of outline. Your documentary filmmaker, in consultation with the principals of the project, may have even completed a treatment. It is now time to work on the first formal script and, to be more specific, what some documentarians call the "shooting script."

As we related in the Introduction, back in 2004, when Pepe Productions began working on the 2005-released documentary *The Lost Radeau: North America's Oldest Intact Warship*, the synergy for beginning that phase of the project came from John Whitesel, a skilled animator who had worked previously with Pepe Productions on corporate videos. Whitesel approached Peter and Joseph Pepe (Pepe Productions) with the documentary idea. Peter was already familiar with the topic, since in the early 1990s, Joseph W. Zarzynski, Russell P. Bellico, and Bob Benway had discussed with him the possibility of doing a documentary on their recent shipwreck discovery, the 1758 *Land Tortoise* radeau shipwreck in Lake George, New York. Its history and uniqueness, the only radeau-class shipwreck ever to have been found, made it an ideal subject for a documentary. In the early 1990s, Zarzynski wrote an outline for the documentary, but the timing was just not right to go into production, and thus the project did not get off the ground. However, thirteen years later and after Whitesel's timely 2004 suggestion, Peter Pepe went to his filing cabinet and found a copy of the original documentary outline prepared by Zarzynski in the early 1990s. Whitesel and Zarzynski, who became the co-scriptwriters for the final production, were able to easily progress into writing a shooting script and then an editing script. Though the production team did not have formal financial backing for making the feature-length documentary, the Pepe Productions team was able to work on the documentary film during evenings and other free time. *The Lost Radeau: North America's Oldest Intact Warship*, 57 minutes long, was completed in just eighteen months. It was directed and edited by Peter Pepe. Zarzynski, an underwater archaeologist on the 1758 *Land Tortoise* radeau study, worked with Pepe throughout the documentary filmmaking process to give advice and check facts on archaeological accuracy. The documentary was released for home video distribution. One reason the crew was able to get the project done in a relatively short eighteen months was that an outline had initially been drafted thirteen years earlier; this, combined with Whitesel's initial draft of a preliminary script, allowed the shooting script to quickly take shape. After shooting the interviews and B-roll, the editing script was promptly drafted. Our point is that, early on, an outline was on paper, and it was not just an idea in the heads of the documentarians. There are countless documentary ideas out there, but not many make it to the end, to a completed documentary.

So, you are several weeks into the project and you have your beginning-middle-end story idea and possibly even an outline. The next step is to come up with a first script, a shooting script. Here is where you should look at the documentary film from two aspects—the visual and the story idea line. Whether you are brainstorming from outline to first script on a yellow pad of lined paper or working on your computer using word processing software, you need to get things written down. So, divide your paper down the middle. Here is where you have an option.

One format for a draft of the shooting script uses the following template. On the left side of your paper, you will have your "Visual" category; and on the right side you will have your "Story Idea Line" headline. Another format for laying out your shooting script—one that we prefer for archaeology-related documentaries—is somewhat different. On the left side of your paper is the "Visual" and on the right side is the "Audio." The difference between the two is that in the latter, the audio description is a full commentary.

We prefer the second format, the Visual/Audio, because we think it enables you to get a better understanding of the documentary. In most cases, the audio half of your paper will be more detailed at first, often with the visual side just a brief description. If you have initial problems in developing this script, take a step back and consider these questions:

- What are the main points you are trying to get across?
- How will you open the documentary?
- Is your documentary using a chronological progression or a crisis, conflict, and resolution progression, or is your documentary progression "the search"?
- How will you eventually come to the climax of your documentary?

The order of your sequences and the segues between them are very important to the weaving together of elements in this first draft. Try to link and connect your sequences so there is a smooth flow throughout the whole documentary. By the same token, since today's technology makes nonlinear editing easy—unlike in the old days using analog when editing had to proceed in production order—you do not necessarily have to decide first about how you are going to open your documentary. You can always come back and change the opening. When you get into your editing script, the draft after the shooting script, your writing team will be able to move sequences around and reorder them into a coherent whole.

After you have completed your shooting script and before you go into the field for production, you will use the shooting script to develop what the director calls the "**shot list**." This lets the director and cameraman know exactly what needs to be shot: the interviews and B-roll footage. The director will rely on this to plan out how to acquire the shots, the scenes, and the sequences. In the next chapter, we will have more to say about the shot list, including an example.

Generally speaking, a documentary is made up of shots, scenes, and sequences. There are several shots in a scene. A scene is one location, and several shots and scenes make up a sequence. The director is the expert in this realm, so he or she will guide you.

Also, if you are including scenes of archaeological fieldwork, be sure to convey to the director what rules of professional archaeological etiquette need to be observed by the crew at an archaeological site, and what specific people, things, and events need to be shot for inclusion in the documentary.

Later in the book (Chapter 14), we will show how the shooting script is transformed into the editing script.

12
PREPRODUCTION—
PRODUCTION COSTS, FUNDING,
ASSEMBLING THE CREW,
COMPILING THE SHOT LIST, AND ON AND ON

I N ALMOST ANY KIND OF PROJECT, successful pre-event planning and logistics coordination generally reap dividends in the end. Not surprisingly, so it is with the preproduction stage in documentary filming. This chapter focuses on the many components you'll have to deal with in the preproduction stage—calculating production costs, finding funding sources, acquiring permissions and permits, drafting release forms, developing the shooting schedule, compiling the all-important shot list, using **storyboards** (if desired), and assembling the production crew.

Production Costs for Making a Documentary

Every single veteran archaeologist I know thinks they have worked on at least one archaeology project that merits some type of documentary, whether for television broadcast, theatrical release, home video distribution, museum screening, or simply to be shown on YouTube or other Internet venues. The constraining factor is, more often than not, money. Somewhere down the road, therefore, if you are seeking a documentary project with a professional production company, the issue of

Documentary Filmmaking for Archaeologists, by Peter Pepe and Joseph W. Zarzynski, 87–100. © 2012 Left Coast Press, Inc. All rights reserved.

funding will be at the top of the list of factors to consider. What, we are always asked, is the basic cost for a making a documentary?

To determine the actual final cost of making a documentary-style production, expenses must be itemized. However, an estimate, or ballpark figure, can certainly be projected, as is often done as a starting price before negotiating a final figure. To determine this ballpark figure, documentary filmmakers may generalize production fees in terms of cost per production minute. Depending on the extent of travel and other relevant expenditures and fees, the overall production cost will probably run about $1,500 to $5,000 per production minute or more (in 2012 U.S. dollars). The "more" part of this estimate is expectable when you are dealing with a major production company with lots of personnel, when you anticipate major travel costs for moving the crew from location to location, and when there will be animation costs. For example, say that you want to make a short documentary production for screening in the local museum's small auditorium to inform patrons about a new exhibit. The museum director, its board, and you have jointly decided you want a professional-looking and quality documentary that is about eight minutes long. This will be shown as an introduction for a major new museum exhibition. If you approach a small local production company, you are probably looking at about $14,000 and up, and more likely in the $17,500–$20,000 range. The final production cost will be more if you want animation, or if substantial traveling is required for shooting the interviews and B-roll. If you are contracting the job to a large and well-known production company, the production cost will probably be substantially higher. Furthermore, if you want 1,000–2,000 copies of the exhibition DVD for resale in the museum gift shop, the museum will also have to pay for DVD replication expenses.

As the principal archaeologist for the archaeology-related documentary, you will confer with the video production company's business manager or director to determine a final figure for the production cost. To negotiate a cost-effective deal, you should be prepared to discuss the following items of the budget (Hampe 2007:380–389):

- General production company expenses for the producer and director, including office costs, transportation, legal fees, various types of insurance, and payroll expenditures

- Preproduction expenses, such as research, scriptwriting, production planning, casting, location logistics, and travel

- Production expenses, such as the crew's salary, possible equipment rental, location fees, and costs for talent, audio, lighting, transportation, lodging, per diem meals, reenactment wardrobe, supplies, and contingencies

- Postproduction expenses, such as review of footage, editing, animation and other computer-generated effects, music, voice talent including narration, sound and video sweetening, poster and graphics design, and website design and hosting

- If needed, distribution expenses such as DVD replication and product shipping

- Possible marketing expenses, such as film festival costs, and newspaper, magazine, and radio advertising

Having an understanding beforehand of the nuances of typical industry costs will certainly aid in keeping costs down and may even improve the quality of the final production.

Funding Sources

Often you will have to search for some source of funding if you are going to get your documentary completed, whether you require a minimal or substantial amount of money. Many television stations—for example, Discovery Communications, History/AETV, and others—will generally only work with experienced producers, so you should align yourself with such a production person or company if possible. If you plan to work with a production company to approach a commissioning editor of a major television company, then you may not need to have money in hand, as the television station will purchase the production. However, if your documentary is intended for a small audience—say, you need to raise money to produce a DVD for sale to generate income for your museum or historical society, or your documentary will only be screened in a museum or historical society—then you will need funds to pay for the cost of hiring a video production company to make the DVD documentary.

In this latter case, let's say you want to make a short documentary to be screened in a museum to complement a new exhibit. What do you have to have in hand when you approach investors or foundations seeking documentary production funding? A portfolio. If you have already met with a production company and have established a collaborative partnership, then the company's director or business manager can work with you to create that portfolio. Below is a list of the basic components your funding-seeking portfolio should include (whether in hard copy or digital format for e-mailing) (Lindenmuth 2010:61). Once complete, you will utilize this in pursuit of funding from foundations and other investors.

■ Your documentary proposal, which presents a synopsis of the documentary, estimated budget total, audience, production company principals, people to be interviewed, documentary approach, and other relevant sections (see Chapter 8)

■ An itemized budget for the documentary

■ The target outlet for your proposed documentary (PBS, local television, museum, historical society, film festival, DVD for resale, etc.)

■ Samples of the production company's previous work (sample documentaries, etc.)

■ Contact information for the project principal

Once the production company gets approval from a television channel's commissioning editor, or once your project has secured the needed funding from a foundation or private investor to move ahead in shooting your documentary, the production team is ready to progress into the later phases of preproduction: assembling the rest of the documentary crew, working out the location logistics, securing permits, permissions, and insurance, drafting project-specific release forms, scheduling production shooting, compiling the shot list, and, if you plan to use one, developing a storyboard. Here are some of the things you might have to know related to each of these.

Assembling the Documentary Filmmaking Crew

Assembling the documentary filmmaking crew is as critical to the documentary production's success as selecting members to a sports team is crucial to winning. The director normally chooses the documentary film crew. Yet, the archaeologist in the documentary collaboration, who probably will serve as a technical advisor, may even be a co-writer, and quite possibly even a producer, needs to be aware of who these people are, what roles they play, and what their personalities are like. The documentary crew, like any experienced archaeology team, starts out as individuals working at their respective jobs, and hopefully they soon mesh into an elite unit to accomplish the project's goals.

What positions does the typical documentary production crew need to fill? Documentary production crews tend to include only a handful of people, unlike well-financed movies that seem to have an army of workers. Documentary production crewmembers often wear many hats, doing multiple tasks. The basic documentary filmmaking crew will probably consist of three to five people. As the production progresses, more people, often contract employees, will be needed to do such jobs as research, acquiring archival film, video footage, and photographs, locating reenactment and talent actors, and the like. So, eventually there may be more people involved in the project, but usually not during initial production shooting. Here is a brief list of crew positions. As noted above, some crewmembers in the project may play multiple roles.

Executive Producer
There is some debate as to the actual role of the executive producer. However, the executive producer is generally the key financial supporter of the endeavor but is not responsible for the day-to-day decisions of the project.

Producer
The documentary producer is responsible for hiring the crew and overseeing the day-to-day budget concerns. The producer works closely with the executive producer and the director.

Director
The job of the documentary director is to fashion the vision for the production and to ensure that high standards are maintained during all stages of the filmmaking. The director will tell the cameraperson how he/she wants the interview and B-roll shot and will work with the scriptwriter and editor.

Scriptwriter

As the title denotes, the scriptwriter will work on one or more of the various versions of the script, possibly even from as early as the original idea, to the outline, to the shooting script, and then the final editing script.

Production Assistant

The unsung heroes of the documentary filmmaking crew are the production assistants. These could be college interns, interested friends, or people who simply want to learn the field of documentary filmmaking from the ground up. The P.A., as they are most often called, performs a variety of tasks, from making sure that talent releases are completed, to making coffee and food runs, to doing photocopying, reminding people (by phone, e-mail, or text) of the details of the production schedule, and any other "grunt work." P.A.s are invaluable members of the crew and often do not even get paid.

Production Manager

The production manager's job is to give support to the director, doing various tasks to ensure a smoothly running production. They routinely undertake the chores of daily production scheduling and location logistics.

Editor

Following production shooting, a talented and experienced post-production editor is crucial to the final look of the documentary. The editor lays in the audio tracks. The editor fashions or edits the shots into sequences to tell the story. A veteran editor can often perform "magic" with digital editing software.

Music Director

The job of the music director is to hunt down original and/or **production music** that is suitable for the tone of the documentary. It is said, and accurately so, that a documentary is mostly a visual experience. Music nonetheless gives feeling and emotion to the documentary, and it should not be underestimated. The archaeologist can work with the music director, editor, and director to listen to some of the selected production music and then offer input as to its potential for the documentary. Satisfying background music can play a critical role in a documentary production.

Narrator

A great narration voice is worth its proverbial weight in gold. There are many wonderful television and documentary narration voices that we have enjoyed over the decades—examples include Rod Serling, James Earl Jones, Sir Richard Attenborough, Peter Coyote, Morgan Freeman, Mike Rowe, and Alec Baldwin, among others. One of the best from the past actually came from the world of sports. Legendary sports broadcaster John Facenda, who for years did narration for NFL Films until his death in the mid-1980s, was so good at his craft that he was often called the "Voice of God" (Teague 2007). Having a great narrator can really help to make a first-rate documentary. To find narration talent that is affordable to the low-budget documentary production, simply Google "voice talent" or "voice-over talent" to check out the numerous websites that offer narration for hire.

Computer Animator/Computer Images Technician

Most archaeology and history documentaries require the use of some type of animation or computer-generated images, since such documentaries are about the past and archival imagery is often not readily available. More and more colleges and universities, and facilities like the D.A.V.E. (digital animation and visual effects) School based in Orlando, Florida, are training accomplished animators. Your director will probably know several animators and computer image technicians. At Pepe Productions, we were fortunate to work with a very talented animator who knew the basics of ship construction and water movement and was able to create realistic animations of historic vessels and shipwrecks. However, animation is expensive, and it can easily chew up funds for a low-budget documentary.

Sound Sweetener

Just after the first cut of the documentary has been completed and before the "doc" is finalized, the director may send the production out for what is called "sound sweetening." A sound sweetener specializes in making the audio sound as high quality as possible.

Documentary directors try to record the best possible sound during production—that is, when the film or video is being shot. But good-quality sound is not always achievable in the field, and some post-production audio work is often necessary. This is where recordings of ambient sounds can be important. **Ambient sound**, otherwise referred to as "natural" sound or "nat" sound, is the background noise that is present before any acting, speaking, or interviews are recorded. This could be something as simple as a gentle breeze or as complex as machinery operating nearby. It can also be hums or low-level noise from any number of sources that you cannot control or subdue easily. If you are not familiar with sound editing, it may surprise you to know that recordings of site-specific ambient sounds can help in postproduction to filter out those same sounds from your interviews and B-roll when they interfere with your audio. So, when the crew is about to begin shooting at a remote location, it is a good idea to record at least a few minutes of ambient sound from the location of each shoot. When the cameras are moved from one location to another within the shooting area, you will realize that the "nat" sounds do change from one place or room to another in the same proximity. The editor or engineer uses these recorded natural sounds during the sound sweetening stage of postproduction. These recordings allow the engineer to isolate the background noise and filter it or eliminate it from the final mix-down without having to separate it from recordings that also include spoken lines or sounds generated by the on-camera talent. The engineer can adjust a filter to control the background noise and then apply a clone of that filter to the actual scenes that are used, resulting in a cleaner audio track that is easier to hear and understand.

Prior to the digital revolution, audio labs for sound sweetening work were generally found only in big entertainment production cities like New York and Los Angeles. More recently, however, such facilities have downsized due to computer advancements (thus needing fewer people), and many have moved to lower-rent facilities all around the country. You would be surprised at the number of sound sweeteners that can be contracted for a few thousand dollars and may possibly be located in your region, too. Clear audio, like good-looking video, certainly helps to create a professional-quality production. Make sure you inquire with your director to see if the production company can hire some type of sound sweetening for your documentary. It will be money well spent.

Video Sweetener

Just as sound sweetening is nowadays a necessity, so too is finding a video sweetener. That person's job is to give the production color balance or color correction so that there is consistency in the documentary's look as it moves from shot to shot and sequence to sequence. Such adjustments may not be readily obvious and may even be subliminal, but beautiful video, like terrific audio, produces a professional-quality appearance.

Location Logistics

If you have ever helped plan the logistics of an out-of-state archaeology excavation—say, in northern New Mexico on an Anasazi site—you are fully aware of all the logistical details that had to be handled to conduct your archaeology fieldwork. Someone had to see to the research design, the excavation permits, formal permissions from landowners, insurance, liability release forms, medical forms for the personnel, college credits for student fieldwork, housing and meals, contingency plans, and on and on. Likewise, the documentary location manager has to deal with similar logistical hurdles when planning and scheduling.

Permits, Permissions, Insurance, and Release Forms

During the preproduction stage, the archaeologist should probably talk to the director and/or location manager to review permits, permissions, insurance, and release forms. Insurance is an important concern to documentarians. Some small production companies may not carry any insurance. Others will do so. Some documentary filmmakers will have liability insurance, production insurance for the safety of the crew, and production equipment insurance. Documentary filmmakers will also probably want to get errors and omissions insurance, which insures the filmmakers from slander, breach of contract on the part of a person in the documentary, and copyright infringement, among other things (Rosenthal 2007:136–137). It is always a smart idea for the archaeologist to ask the director or production manager what type of insurance they have and what it actually covers.

If the documentarian plans to shoot interviews and acquire B-roll of your archaeological excavation, you will need to confer and coordinate these activities with him or her. It will be up to you to inform the documentarian of what the crew can and cannot shoot, based on the archaeological sensitivities and protocols in that environment. Explain the basic archaeological etiquette. The director or the director's P.A. will have re-lease forms for the archaeology team members and for others to sign. Typically, these are **location releases** and **personal/video releases**.

A location release is a form that grants formal permission to shoot on private property. If this form is needed in your case, it should be signed days before going into the field.

Everyone on camera will be required to sign a personal/video re-lease form. If it is possible to do so, the archaeologist should get a copy of this form ahead of time and review it with the archaeology team members. Then the P.A. will get everyone to sign an individual copy. Sometimes during interviews, the production unit will also require what is called a "**video release**." This is a formal release to use the in-terview, issued via videotape showing interviewees giving their permis-sion. In many respects, it is best to get both the written and video releases. The documentarian will know if other permissions or releases are required. These might include a minor release, to be signed by a parent or legal guardian of a minor who will appear on camera; a tal-ent release, when professional actors are utilized in the documentary; and a materials release, to obtain permission to use copyrighted media like video, film, and photographs.

The archaeologist should also get a liability release form signed by each of the production crewmembers who will be in the field. This all is quite a "paper shuffle," but nowadays this is obligatory paperwork.

Film Commission

Many locales where a documentary is being shot will have a **film com-mission**. These are quasi-governmental, not-for-profit groups that work with filmmakers and documentarians to assist with on-site logis-tics, finding affordable housing and office space, troubleshooting loca-tion problems, assisting in acquiring various permits, and other similar tasks. Your director will probably check to see if the location where your documentary is being shot has such a film commission. If so, film com-missions should be contacted during the preproduction planning, be-fore the documentary crew goes into the field. A film commission can be an invaluable asset during production work and even later, during marketing of the completed documentary.

Scheduling Shooting

During preproduction, the director will schedule the shooting of the interviews and the acquisition of B-roll. This can happen in one of two ways. Either the director will tell the archaeologist when he or she will bring the production crew into the field and when interviews will be shot, or the archaeologist will inform the director of the most suitable time to come into the field to acquire the most dramatic and illustrative B-roll. Regardless of who schedules the production shooting, it is necessary to plan for "Mr. Murphy" lurking around. A documentary crew cannot get good footage during inclement weather, so you always need a "Plan B," a contingency strategy for bad weather and unexpected hurdles. In many cases, the director or the production's location manager may want to visit the archaeological site prior to bringing the documentary crew out. It's a good idea for the archaeologist to invite the director out into the field and for the two of you to discuss logistics and the shooting schedule. One way or another, the director will have a shooting schedule set up in advance that tells exactly what day(s) to shoot, specific times, and what is to be shot (shot list). Even the best-devised shooting schedule cannot be realized without reminding everyone of the schedule. That gentle e-mail reminder sent out a couple of days ahead of time will help keep "Mr. Murphy" away from your documentary project.

Compiling the Shot List

The director is responsible for examining the shooting script and then preparing a shot list for the interviews and B-roll. While it differs from documentary to documentary, generally speaking the ratio of recorded video or film time to the actual production duration is about 6:1 to 10:1 or more. Of course, the ratio can vary greatly. For our documentary *Search for the* Jefferson Davis: *Trader, Slaver, Raider*, we shot nine hours of B-roll, and the documentary runs just short of an hour. It is really hard to pinpoint a standard ratio because some crews shoot with multiple cameras simultaneously. We have done some research among producer groups, and the consensus is that there is no standard ratio. They all say that it depends on the project.

Peter Pepe, an experienced documentary director says, "My biggest concern is that we don't want to give the impression that one has to shoot lots of film or video footage to make a good documentary. Just shooting footage for the sake of shooting footage is rather ridiculous. Someone has to spend huge amounts of time to catalog it and transcribe interviews, and that is rather dumb if they are doing it just to have lots of footage. It's the quality of the footage that counts."

In some cases, the director may wish to shoot some of the interviews in the field rather than in an office setting. This can be problematic, especially if the location is an archaeological site next to a highway with lots of traffic noise or if the site is adjacent to construction work, a situation that is quite common during cultural resource management (CRM) fieldwork.

As an example of a shot list for B-roll, Table 12.1 presents part of a shot list we used during production work on our documentary *Wooden Bones: The Sunken Fleet of 1758*. For each shot, we describe what video footage (B-roll) is desired, the kind of camera shot (wide, medium, or closeup), whether the camera for the shot is handheld or utilizes a tripod, and the number of minutes of B-roll required.

Later on in the book (see Chapter 13), we will offer insight into the art of interviews and suggest how to optimize the interview process so that the archaeologist, when interviewed, really sounds like an expert and gives superb **sound bites**.

Storyboards

Some directors like to use storyboards to advise both the crew and actors (or reenactors) how best to visualize the look of a scene. Storyboards are sort of like a comic book, graphic novel, or slide show of individual shots, each sketched in a separate frame and annotated to give further direction. A documentary director who has some artistic talent may utilize storyboards using his or her own artwork. These can be simple drawings; even stick-figure sketches can convey the gist of a scene. Storyboards are sometimes used in history-related documentaries where actors or reenactments are required and the director needs to tell the talent what to do and also direct the crew in how he or she wants to shoot it. Of course, many archaeologists are accomplished artists, having

Table 12.1. Shot List for *Wooden Bones: The Sunken Fleet of 1758*

1	B-roll	The vessel, *TuffBoat*, tied up to a mooring at The Sunken Fleet of 1758 shipwreck preserve, Lake George, New York	Wide shot and medium shot; videography shot from Wiawaka Holiday House onshore looking out to the watercraft just offshore; use tripod for camera shots; 2 minutes
2	B-roll	Bateaux Below dive team members loading scuba gear onto the dive vessel *TuffBoat*	Medium shots and closeup shots, B-roll shot from various angles; use handheld and tripod camera shots; 4 minutes
3	B-roll	French and Indian War re-enactment at Battlefield Park, Lake George, New York	Wide shots, medium shots, and closeup shots of colonial soldiers (British and French) and Native American reenactors in camp and also fighting; make sure there are no traffic signposts, cars, SUVs, telephone poles, and other modern items in the video footage; use handheld and tripod camera shots; 5 minutes
4	B-roll	Aboard the vessel *TuffBoat*	Wide shots and closeup shots of scuba divers entering the lake from the boat, divers in the water on the lake surface, divers about to descend, dive boat flag fluttering in the breeze, etc.; use handheld camera shots; 5 minutes
5	B-roll	Exhibits in the Lake George Historical Association museum related to shipwrecks and underwater archaeology	Wide shots and closeups of display cases, artifacts on exhibition, and exhibit signage all associated with "The Sunken Fleet of 1758"; use camera mounted on a tripod; 5 minutes
6	B-roll	Members of Bateaux Below sinking a replica bateau in the shallows of Lake George in June 2009 to create a "shipwreck exhibit" for pedestrian viewing	Wide shots, medium shots, and closeup shots using a tripod; 5 minutes

drawn artifacts, maps, and the like. So, do not be shy. If you think a reenactment scene or B-roll should be shot a certain way, suggest it to the director by laying it out in storyboard format. Figure 12.1 shows a sample of a storyboard scene constructed from *Search for the Jefferson Davis: Trader, Slaver, Raider*. Today, it is relatively easy to create professional-looking storyboards using specialized computer software. The Internet is a good place to look for software that offers this capability.

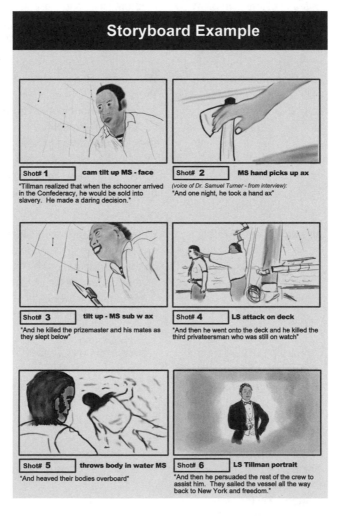

Figure 12.1: This is an example of a storyboard constructed by documentarian Peter Pepe. Storyboards are drawings or sketches that are annotated with directional notes that serve as planning aids for the documentary crew, talent, and interviewees during production shooting (*credit: Peter Pepe*).

13

THE ART OF
THE INTERVIEW AND B-ROLL

TWO OF THE BIGGEST UNDERTAKINGS FOR DOCUMENTARY filmmaking teams are (1) acquiring great interviews with terrific sound bites and (2) shooting illustrative B-roll. Both are integral to telling the production's story. As a principal in the production team, the archaeologist will most likely be called upon to:

1. be interviewed,

2. help draft some of the questions used in the numerous interviews, and

3. offer expert advice on what archaeology-related B-roll should be shot during production for usage by the editor in postproduction.

This chapter provides insight into attaining informative interviews and representative B-roll.

The Interview

During preproduction, a list of possible interviewees will be drawn up, and it is likely that the production's archaeologist will have considerable input into who is on this register. After the list of interviewees has been finalized, several pre-interview tasks should be done.

Documentary Filmmaking for Archaeologists, by Peter Pepe and Joseph W. Zarzynski, 101–108. © 2012 Left Coast Press, Inc. All rights reserved.

Preparing the Interviewee

Phone calls and e-mails are directed to potential interviewees to determine if they will agree to be interviewed. During the phone calls, e-mails, and the pre-interview meetings, several topics may be addressed. Here not only do the interviewee and interviewer get to know each other, they also review ground rules, agree on a location for the interview, and perhaps even discuss what the interviewee should and should not wear (see list below).

Characteristics of Clothing to Avoid in an Interview

Here are some suggestions on what not to wear for an interview:

1. If possible, avoid wearing white clothing, as it sometimes becomes too noticeable or bright on screen.

2. Avoid wearing black clothes, since they need more lighting to show up on video.

3. Avoid wearing red, pin stripes, checks, and herringbone patterns. The stripes and checks often seem to vibrate on screen, which is very distracting.

The interviewer will offer a few tips to the interviewee—suggesting, for example, that, whenever possible, the answer to a question should include a rephrasing of the question, as that will edit down into a better sound bite. At this meeting, however, it is very important that the interviewee and interviewer not get too involved in the details of what specific questions will be asked—mainly because a director wants unrehearsed answers, compelling sound bites filled with unrehearsed emotion. If an interviewee asks for the questions ahead of time, rather than provide that list of questions, the interviewer might just pass along some general talking points. In that way, the interviewee can research the topics to be discussed in the interview, but not specifically rehearse answers that can come across as prepared replies and thus mundane sound bites.

As noted, the ground rules may be discussed at this time. The interviewer may want assurances that there will be no interruptive noise while the interviewee is on standby, such as idle chatter in a nearby room or cell phones ringing. Likewise, many documentary directors do not want any outside audience present, such as friends or family members, who can sometimes distract the interviewee.

Determining the Interview Location

The location for an interview is critical. Sometimes the director will want to scout potential locations for interviews, to see if the locale's environment fits the slant and mood of the documentary. Moreover, the location must be a place that will feel comfortable to the interviewee. A person inexperienced in being interviewed might be a bit daunted by the atmosphere in a studio filled with lights, cameras, and a production crew. In that case, consider a more casual environment, which may result in a better interview with more usable sound bites.

Another point to consider is whether to shoot the interview inside or outside. If inside, choose a spot that does not have windows with sun pouring into a room. Stay away from a room with a tile floor that can be noisy, with sounds of people and equipment being shuffled around. An inside location might require lights, too. Of course, outside locations also have their downside. An archaeological site might be an ideal place for an interview, but potential problems include ambient noise from archaeological diggers, mechanical equipment being used, or loud vehicular traffic next to a site. And sometimes the location simply does not add to the mood of the documentary. These are all things the director will contemplate before making the final call on interview locations. Nonetheless, the archaeologist should consider all these points, too, and should take the initiative to offer expert advice to the director.

Camera Setup

Once it is time to do the interview, the director will decide on the camera setup. Generally speaking, there are three types of camera configurations for an interview:

1. The interviewee looks directly into the camera.

2. The camera is positioned so that the interviewee appears to be conversing with a person to the left or right of the camera.

3. The interviewer will be seen on camera along with the interviewee.

Figure 13.1: When conducting a video interview, the camera and interviewee setup is critical. One of the most popular techniques for these interviews is to have the camera positioned so that the interviewee appears to be in conversation with a person (interviewer) to the left or right of the camera, as shown in this photograph (*credit: courtesy of Champlain Stone, Ltd.*).

In most cases, setup 2 is chosen, and it is the type most often preferred by Pepe Productions and many other documentary production crews (Figure 13.1).

Releases and Identifications

As noted in Chapter 12, prior to the interview, the director must have in hand a formal written release signed by the interviewee. If a video release is also needed, the camera will roll as the interviewee states his or her name and then gives permission to use the interview in the documentary. We like to get a written release and then record a video release.

Next, the interviewee is asked to pronounce his or her name to get the correct pronunciation. The interviewer also asks how the interviewee would like his or her name to appear on the screen. Finally, the interviewee is asked how he or she wants to be identified—for example, as Archaeologist, Project Director, Project Manager, or Cultural Resource Manager. Surprisingly, this simple question can sometimes be problematic, as some people cannot quickly decide how they want to be identified. During the pre-interview telephone call, you might want to ask the interviewee how he or she wants to be identified on screen. Generally, the people being interviewed are selected because they are experts in their field. Therefore, their title should reflect the image the documentary team is trying to get across. For example, in our 2005 documentary, *The Lost Radeau: North America's Oldest Intact Warship*, we interviewed Martin Klein, who has often been called "The Father of Commercial Side-Scan Sonar" and "The Godfather of Side-Scan Sonar." So, on screen we identified him as "Sonar Pioneer," an accurate appellation that just oozed with authority.

Conducting the Interview

Now it is time for the interview. In a low-budget archaeology-related documentary with only the director as principal cameraperson, the archaeologist may be drafted into doing some of the interviews. So, here is some upfront advice on conducting an interview. The first question that is asked of the interviewee is rather important. You want it to be an easy question to build the confidence of the interviewee. You might want to open some questions with the words "Tell me about...." When conducting the interview in camera setup 2 (see p. 103), it is essential that the interviewer maintain eye contact with the interviewee and show genuine interest in what the interviewee is saying. This will help elicit solid replies and usable sound bites.

A veteran interviewer will know when to rephrase a question to get a better response. If, during the course of the interview, the interviewee veers off in an unexpected direction with an answer, it is sometimes acceptable to proceed in that direction, in order to get a fresh perspective on a topic. Finally, when the interviewer has finished with the list of questions, the interviewee should always be asked if there is anything he or she wishes to add. You would be surprised at some of the amazing sound bites you get from that final response, many of which do end up in the documentary. An accomplished interviewer will try to make the interview a conversation rather than an interrogation. The interviewee will appreciate fairness and sensitivity on the part of the production crew, too. Likewise, refrain from putting words into the mouth of the interviewee, and do not interrupt unless the interviewee drifts too far off the subject being discussed.

Now it is time to coach the archaeologist if he or she is going to be interviewed for the documentary. The truth is that archaeologists and historians do not always give outstanding interviews. They certainly know their topic well, so what are the problems? Check out our list (see below) of things to consider if you, the archaeologist or historian, are being interviewed.

Tips for a Giving a Good Interview

1. Be enthusiastic. You are the expert, so show that.

2. Do not get bogged down with too many details. This is one of the biggest problems that can confront a documentary film crew when interviewing experts. It is better for the archaeologist or historian to generalize and give a succinct reply than to give a long and boring discourse.

3. Stay away from words like "it," "them," and "they." Identify what these things are and who these people are.

4. Try to talk without being too technical.

5. Try to keep your answers short and to the point.

6. If you start an answer and stumble, simply ask the documentary crew if you can restart your reply to the question.

B-Roll

Once the interview has been shot, the director will inform the camera crew to go out and shoot B-roll. Acquiring illustrative B-roll footage is a mainstay of documentary filmmaking. For example, if an interview has been shot in the office of an archaeologist who works for a university, the B-roll might include:

1. A wide shot of the university campus

2. A closeup shot of the sign in front of the university identifying the institution

3. A wide shot of the specific building where the archaeologist has an office or laboratory

4. Medium shots, closeups, and extreme closeup shots of the archaeologist at work in his or her office or laboratory, examining artifacts or reviewing documents

5. Footage of the archaeologist at a lectern teaching a class or giving a lecture to the public

6. Footage of the archaeologist in the field "doing" archaeology

7. Shots of the archaeology team in the laboratory and in the field "doing" archaeology.

The project archaeologist needs to take the initiative to offer advice to the director on what other B-roll should be acquired to facilitate telling the story. Likewise, the director will probably ask the archaeologist for a CD with photographs showing archaeological fieldwork, laboratory work, artifacts, and the like. These photographs should be high-resolution images, at least 4 MB in size and preferably larger. The images should be in horizontal format, since the medium of documentary filmmaking is horizontal. Vertical photographs are seldom used. All photographs, in digital format and generally as JPEGs, should be labeled, and there should be a detailed description of each describing what is being portrayed.

Special Conditions for Underwater Footage

Shooting underwater photography and B-roll video for maritime and nautical archaeology documentaries poses a unique set of challenges. We have worked with several talented underwater photographers and videographers on our documentaries—Russell P. Bellico, Bob Benway, and Steven C. Resler.

Underwater photography and videography can only be as good as the water is clear. Unlike acquiring photographs and shooting video on land, if the lake or ocean waters are murky, then your images are likely to be rather poor. Underwater lights can illuminate dark waters, but if there is a lot of suspended algae or bottom sediment tossed up in the water column from scuba divers, underwater lights will simply show that backscatter. A single strobe light or pair of strobe lights affixed to an underwater camera really needs to be positioned correctly and have a certain light intensity in order to get optimal results. So, if you plan to use underwater photographers and videographers in your documentary, be aware that sometimes the image quality will be somewhat limited.

Shooting underwater videography at a shipwreck site can be a minefield of potential problems. Scuba divers should not wear white or bright colors, as these can "bloom" when underwater lights hit them or when shooting in shallow water under sunny conditions. Another concern is when an underwater videographer swims along a shipwreck site shooting video. Sometimes the resulting video will rock slightly, back and forth, as the scuba diver kicked with his or her fins. The shakiness of the resulting video image can give some viewers a sense of being seasick.

One way to get professional underwater video results is for the videographer to position him- or herself on the lake bottom or seafloor and then shoot video with slow **panning**. The underwater videographer is essentially acting like a camera and tripod giving stability to the video shot. If an underwater videographer is shooting B-roll of a shipwreck, that person may want to shoot in several locations around the shipwreck, not touching the submerged cultural resource but getting a series of several seconds of each shot. The video results from this process are far better than video that moves or bounces due to diver fin kicks.

Above the water, B-roll of underwater archaeologists loading a boat, of the expedition boat leaving the wharf, of divers and underwater archaeologists planning their dive, gearing up in their scuba suits, entering the water from the boat, and climbing back aboard the dive boat, and the dive boat returning back to the marina, all make for pictorial and exciting B-roll.

Regardless of whether the documentary filmmakers use B-roll (film or video) and/or still photographs, animation, or illustrations, it is imperative that these all serve to illustrate the story being told. A documentary is primarily a visual story, so all these images must be powerful, real, and dramatic (Hampe 2007:109–112).

As you learned in this chapter, the job of the archaeologist who is an integral part of a collaborative archaeology documentary filmmaking team is to advise the director on content, interviews, and what B-roll and other images best tell the documentary story so that it is compelling and truthful.

14
WORK FOLLOWING
THE INTERVIEWS AND B-ROLL

ONCE THE CREW HAS FINISHED SHOOTING all the interviews and B-roll, it is time to see what footage was collected. The director, or possibly the editor, will review the interview and B-roll footage. During this process, the director and/or editor might invite the documentary project archaeologist to participate in **logging footage** and then in rewriting the script to include interviews and narration.

Logging and Transcribing

What is "logging" of film and video footage? Most documentaries today are shot on videotape, and thus there is a **time code** generated on the tapes. Essentially, there are two ways that a documentary team can approach logging footage. One is to review all video and log it—that is, on your computer or on a sheet of paper, you note the time code, description, and possibly even comments on each footage segment. The other approach, taken by some directors and editors, is to discard bad footage and keep and log only video clips of interviews and B-roll that are deemed useful for possible inclusion into the documentary. Regardless of what approach to logging is followed, next the interviews need to be transcribed—that is, a team member listens to the interviews and makes a written copy of exactly what was said. Nowadays this can be accomplished by computer transcription. There is, for example, an incredible speech recognition software program called Dragon Dictation, which recognizes speech and then puts it into written words. There is an app for iPhones and other smart phones, and a more sophisticated version can be purchased for your computer.

The Editing Script

Once your team has logged footage and transcribed the interviews, it is time to rewrite the earlier script into an editing script. The editing script will include narration (if narration is to be used), interview sound bites, and also visuals—B-roll, photographs, illustrations, reenactments, and animation—to illustrate and complement the audio (see Appendix 3 for a sample of an editing script, the opening of *The Lost Radeau: North America's Oldest Intact Warship*). The editing script format we use has two columns, with the video and other visuals described on the left side of the sheet and the audio text on the right. The scriptwriter, in consultation with the director and the producer(s), will write the editing script and then get input from the documentary project archaeologist before going into postproduction editing. The role of the archaeologist is quite important here, as the archaeologist serves as a checker of historical facts, archaeology protocol, and even style of the narration. Many times we have watched a reputedly "good" documentary, movie, or television program on some archaeological topic only to discover the production is loaded with factual and historical mistakes.

To review: The editing script, as noted earlier, is the script used by the editor to fashion or edit the documentary production. The progression toward its development is as follows. The seed for the documentary comes from a single idea. From that seed, the collaborative archaeologist/documentary filmmaker team produces a title and tagline, which evolves into an initial outline, generally a page or two, which shapes the idea into a more concrete story. During these early stages, a lot of research is done. Then the general outline is expanded into a formal documentary proposal, which might also include a separate document, the treatment, which describes the general visual progression of the documentary story. From that, a shooting script is written. When read, it may sound much like narration, but it also includes descriptions of whatever visuals are required. From the shooting script, the director and archaeologist create a shot list before going into the field. Interviews are lined up and shot, and B-roll is collected. Footage is then logged and interviews transcribed. Then the team reviews all the footage (interviews and B-roll,), photographs, illustrations, maps, and any other content. Sometime during these stages, reenactments may be shot and possibly some meetings set up with an animator to discuss animation work. The production principals then write the editing script.

Do not be surprised if the editing script is quite different from the shooting script. It generally is, because surprises almost always crop up during the interview phase, and these will get incorporated into the editing script. As the video editing is being done, the narration script is being polished. Likewise during these stages, a narrator is being selected; and the narration will be recorded for insertion during editing. Of course, this progression can differ from one documentary project to another. During the editing phase, the production may proceed from a rough cut of the documentary to various versions where the production is refined to get to a **fine cut**. Here, tough decisions may need to be made, as some noteworthy footage may have to be deleted to meet the estimated length of the production.

15
CHOOSING THE NARRATOR AND OTHER VOICE TALENT

SELECTING A NARRATOR FOR THE DOCUMENTARY'S voice-over commentary and finding other talent such as character voices to read journal entries are tasks for the documentary filmmaking team principals. To be truly successful, a documentary production needs masterful and appealing sound. In a documentary that uses narration, this element is integral to the whole production, since it ties together the visual images and interviews to tell the story in a smooth, flowing manner. Without great narration, the production can seem choppy, lacking in continuity, and emotionally flat. A powerful narration depends on both a compelling voice and a well-crafted, interesting narration text. Together they draw the audience into the story, enhancing the viewing experience. So, here we will look at how you can compose a successful narration text and find a consummate narrator and other voice talent for your archaeology-related documentary.

Writing the Narration Text

Great wordsmithing is not so easy. It takes talent and skill to craft polished narration. Take a careful study of the thirteen characteristics of well-written narration that should be considered if you are tasked with drafting the narration for your documentary (see the list that follows) (Bernard 2011:205–221).

Characteristics of Good Narration Text

1. Narration breathes life into the B-roll, photographs, illustrations, maps, and animation.

2. Narration does not just describe the visual. It should provide added information about it, too.

3. Narration helps advance the story.

4. Narration should not create a false or misleading impression of the visual content on the screen.

5. Narration should be written to be spoken rather than to be read.

6. Narration tends to use sentences that are shorter than sentences that are read.

7. Narration is written in an active voice.

8. Narration should not be confusing to the viewer.

9. Narration stays away from words that are "tongue twisters."

10. Narration should be grammatically correct.

11. Narration should be gender-neutral. Rather than talk about the fishermen, talk about people fishing.

12. Narration needs to keep the pace of the documentary moving forward.

13. Narration sets the stage for an interviewee's comments.

Finding a Narrator

Besides writing first-class narration, the production team principals need to find an outstanding voice for narration. There are generally five basic things to consider when hunting for your documentary's narrator.

Characteristics of a Good Narration Voice

1. A narrator has a compelling voice that is easy to understand.

2. A narrator's voice fits the content or mood of the documentary.

3. A narrator's voice adds excitement into the documentary.

4. If appropriate to your topic, a narrator's voice may be "localized" to the region of the audience. The popular and highly acclaimed documentary *Planet Earth*, originally a BBC production, used noted British actor David Attenborough for the narration. However, the version shown in the United States on the Discovery Channel used the actress Sigourney Weaver as narrator, to "localize" it for an American viewing audience (Accredited Language Service 2010).

5. A narrator's fee should fit within the documentary production's budget.

In our two Lake George, New York, underwater archaeology DVD documentaries, *The Lost Radeau: North America's Oldest Intact Warship* (2005) and *Wooden Bones: The Sunken Fleet of 1758* (2010), Pepe Productions hired a local voice talent, Kip Grant, as narrator. Grant was an ideal choice. Not only did he have a classic voice for narration, he also had a recognizable voice to folks in the greater Lake George/Glens Falls region. Having spent his professional career doing local radio as well as voice-over work on commercials, his voice was familiar to the audience and helped in creating local buzz for the two productions. Nor did it hurt that a regional radio personality was involved in both projects, as Kip Grant was an admirable ambassador for the documentaries and promoted them over his radio shows, too.

Sometimes a documentary, especially an archaeology documentary that uses journals and diary quotes from the past, may have need for other voice talent besides the narrator. In both of the just-mentioned documentaries, we required voice talent to read excerpts from eighteenth-century historical journals. We were fortunate to find excellent local talent at no cost to our production. In one case, we used a man born in Scotland who had moved to the United States many years earlier but still retained his native accent. In another case, we used a local-area British transplant for more than one voice, and he had some theater experience, too, which was an asset. Voice talent artists who can be utilized for multiple voices can save you time and possibly even money.

Local theater guilds can be a starting point when looking for voice talent. Often, small theater company actors and actresses are elated to do this type of job for free or at a price that will not break your production budget, since this kind of work builds their acting resumes. Alternatively, you can search the Internet using the search words "voice talent" to look for professionals experienced in narration or character voice work. There are numerous websites that not only offer direct contact with voice artists, but also provide the opportunity to put your job out to bid. This works in a very efficient way: you can save time and money by including your own specific criteria—male or female, a specific age range, energy level, and the like—in your request for bids from voice actors. Most professional voice artists take direction very well because they realize that the success of your documentary production reflects directly on how well they did their job.

16
SHOT MAKING

Q UITE OFTEN WHEN WE TEACH OUR WORKSHOP on documentary filmmaking for archaeologists, we get asked questions centered around shooting video to either document fieldwork or to have it available in the future for documentary production work. We have already covered what types of cameras are available. It is now time to offer a few tips on camera shot making.

Buy a Tripod

You may already use a tripod for some of your still photography documentation. Good. If not, go out and buy a quality tripod, one that is sturdy but not too heavy to carry around in the field. It will be money well spent. Make sure the head mount on top of the tripod will receive your video camera. Also, if possible, purchase a tripod that has a bubble balance; this will ensure that your tripod will not be set at a tilted angle in the field, thus ruining your video.

Use Your Tripod

Making shots with a handheld or shoulder-mounted video camera is a skill that normally takes years of practice to learn well. Therefore, make sure you use the tripod whenever you can. Your interviews and B-roll shots using a tripod will be superior to those from handheld and shoulder-mounted cameras (Figure 16.1).

Documentary Filmmaking for Archaeologists, by Peter Pepe and Joseph W. Zarzynski, 117–120. © 2012 Left Coast Press, Inc. All rights reserved.

Know Your Camera and Tripod

Your video camera and its partner, the tripod, are your friends. Take the time to study the camera manual and become adept in its use. The night before you go into the field to shoot video, review the camera manual and practice with the camera and tripod. Your shot making is sure to improve, and you will not look like an amateur in the field.

"Don't Be a Jerk"

That is, learn not to jerk your video camera as you move it, as too much motion ruins the quality of your video. Do not pan quickly from one subject to the next. It is probably best that you be stationary when videotaping, and keep your shot to about 15–20 seconds of stationary B-roll. Likewise, when zooming your camera shot, go slow.

Figure 16.1: Peter Pepe (*left*), director and cameraman, and Chuck Meide (*right*), director of Lighthouse Archaeological Maritime Program, during an interview set up for the production of the documentary *Search for the* Jefferson Davis: *Trader, Slaver, Raider.* Most interviews are shot using a camera mounted onto a tripod to give greater camera stability (*credit: Joseph W. Zarzynski/Pepe Productions*).

Compose Your Camera Shot

Before you start videotaping, take some time to make sure you properly frame the subject in your viewfinder. Your patience will pay off with far better **shot composition**.

Get a Good Microphone

Your on-camera microphone is adequate for picking up ambient sound, but it is not good enough for acquiring professional-sounding interviews. Therefore, purchase a lavalier microphone. This is an independent microphone that clips onto the collar or lapel of the shirt or suit jacket of the person being interviewed. This type of external microphone is not extremely costly, and your audio will sound much more professional.

Lighting

There is a simple rule for an inexperienced video cameraperson. If you do not have professional lighting, then simply shoot in well-lit places.

Outfit Your Video Camera Bag

If you are a dirt archaeologist working on an excavation, you never venture into the field without your dig kit with its trowels, brushes, dustpan, line level, compass, and the other tools of your profession. Likewise, underwater archaeologists have their scuba gear, dive slate and pencil, tape measure, compass, and other recording tools in their mesh bag when mapping shipwrecks. The same should be true for you when you become a video cameraperson. Your video camera bag should have extra batteries, the appropriate camera cables, cassette tapes or whatever other data storage system the camera utilizes, professional tape to secure loose cables to the floor, and so on. Always be prepared, and whenever possible, carry extra accessories.

Catalog Your Video Footage for Future Reference

It is imperative that the video footage be cataloged as soon as possible after it has been recorded. Someone from the field crew must be present when this is done, in order to correctly identify exactly what is in each shot. When creating a video catalog template, we like to include columns for the time code at the beginning of the scene, an abbreviated description of the scene, the date and place of the recording, the video aspect ratio (4:3 or 16:9), and the type of shot (that is, a wide-angle shot, a closeup, a zoom, or a pan). You should also have a column for noting the overall quality of the scene or interview. When cataloging interviews, it is very helpful if you have them transcribed verbatim.

It is a good idea to create your catalog in a common document format such as Microsoft Word or Excel, as this allows users to quickly search for key words that pertain to the scenes they may be looking for.

Cataloging is something that is usually done at the end of the shoot or as soon afterward as possible. It is too easy to forget details about the scenes or interviews, especially when you are shooting on a daily basis. If you wait for days or weeks after shooting to catalog your footage, mislabeling is bound to occur. These catalogs will be an invaluable resource for years to come, so you want them to be accurate.

The tips in this chapter are simple reminders that will make you a better video shot maker.

17
SHOOTING REENACTMENTS
FOR YOUR DOCUMENTARY

SOME ARCHAEOLOGY-, ANTHROPOLOGY-, AND HISTORY-related documentaries might use reenactments, sometimes called "re-creations," in place of standard B-roll. If not overdone, historical reenactments are an excellent way for documentarians to convey their story. Over the years, Pepe Productions has videotaped numerous reenactments of encampments and battle scenes from the French and Indian War (1755–1763) and the American Revolution (1775–1783), with hundreds of reenactors involved in each. Some of this B-roll from French and Indian War reenactments has been incorporated into our documentaries and has proven to be very effective.

Many veteran reenactors have been reliving military battles and camp life for years, and thus they have become rather polished "actors." Most history reenactors welcome a chance to be in a documentary. However, sometimes shooting reenactments, especially battle scenes, can be problematic, particularly if the reenactments are at sites that have visible modern-day features such as power lines, paved roads, street signage, cars and trucks, and eager spectators carrying cameras and pushing baby carriages. Nevertheless, historical reenactments using weekend reenactors—or, better yet, professional actors—can enhance your documentary if they are not overdone.

So, how does a documentary filmmaker shoot historical reenactments using primarily weekend reenactors trying to be as accomplished

Documentary Filmmaking for Archaeologists, by Peter Pepe and Joseph W. Zarzynski, 121–126. © 2012 Left Coast Press, Inc. All rights reserved.

as Hollywood's finest? There are some standard approaches that we all have seen employed many times, such as showing several seconds of B-roll of soldiers' boots as they march, or a military flag blowing in the wind with gun and cannon smoke engulfing it, or a closeup of a single soldier loading his musket and showing his determined and fatigued face. These closeup shots of one or two soldiers, if videotaped correctly, can also project the impression of there being countless soldiers on hand. However, if you include too many of such scenes, they can lose their effectiveness. Then again, sometimes shooting a battle reenactment with hundreds of reenactors simply does not convey a realistic sense of the terror associated with real warfare. So, occasionally in our use of battle scenes or other historical reenactments, we have had to add sepia tone and other video effects to the footage to give it that old "look and feel."

There are other things to watch out for when videotaping historical reenactments of battle scenes. One time during a French and Indian War reenactment at Battlefield Park in Lake George, New York, among several British and provincial soldiers standing and kneeling close together loading their muskets, a reenactor in a group being videotaped pulled out a pocket-size digital camera from under his uniform jacket. The reenactor then quickly snapped a photograph of the "enemy" in front of him. He was so unassuming and agile with this move that the B-roll footage actually made it into the documentary's rough cut version before it was detected during one of the many fact-check screenings. The point is: if you shoot historical reenactments, make sure your editor spends a lot of time checking and rechecking your B-roll as it is being logged or in the rough cuts. A goof like that could have been a catastrophic for the authenticity of our documentary.

In Pepe Productions' documentary *Search for the* Jefferson Davis—*Trader, Slaver, Raider*, we had to do three historical reenactments from the Civil War (1861–1865) era. In one case, we enlisted an experienced Union solder reenactor from Saratoga County, New York, named Chris Heidorf. We shot B-roll of him loading and firing his musket and also videotaped other Civil War–period military scenes with him. Not only was Heidorf very professional, he dressed in authentic time-period garb, was entirely realistic, and was also absolutely ecstatic to assist our production. To top off his superb contribution to our project, he charged us nothing for his time and professional services.

In another case for the same documentary, we had to reenact a more complex and involved historical scene, the 1861 event of African-American steward William Tillman recapturing the Long Island–built schooner *S. J. Waring* after the trading vessel had been seized by Confederate privateers from the brig *Jefferson Davis*. This scene was shot on the edge of a marina in St. Augustine, Florida, in sweltering heat. The weather made it tough for our two reenactors, both of whom were dressed mostly in wool, a common material for sailors in the 1860s (Figure 17.1). We got incredible assistance for this shoot from the underwater archaeology not-for-profit corporation named LAMP (Lighthouse Archaeological Maritime Project) and their associate not-for-profit corporation, the St. Augustine Lighthouse & Museum. Both

Figure 17.1: Reenactors Brendan Burke (*left*) and James Bullock (*right*), during videotaping of the historical reenactment of William Tillman, an African-American steward, retaking the schooner *S. J. Waring* from Confederate privateersmen. Tillman killed several privateersmen and then, with help from some crewmembers, sailed the previously captured prize to New York City. Tillman then became a hero in the North. Historical reenactments are often used in archaeology documentaries (*credit: Emily Jane Murray/Pepe Productions*).

organizations and their respective directors, underwater archaeologist Chuck Meide and Lighthouse Museum Executive Director Kathy Fleming, and their staff were instrumental in lining up a replica nineteenth-century sailing vessel, period-looking wooden casks from a local winery, a small replica of a period-looking wooden rowboat, and a trunk full of Civil War–era replica clothing. We also succeeded in getting a local reenactor, James Bullock, to portray William Tillman and then got LAMP underwater archaeologist Brendan Burke, a dead-ringer for Johnny Depp, to play a Confederate privateer. Burke had done some previous reenacting, too, portraying historical sailors. So, both Bullock and Burke were excellent candidates for director Peter Pepe to work with during the reenactment production shoot. In another short reenactment for that documentary, we had access to one of the small boats built by the St. Augustine Lighthouse & Museum's boat builders. The historically accurate watercraft held reenactors who portrayed privateers bringing ashore some of the captured goods from the brig *Jefferson Davis* after it grounded and was abandoned off St. Augustine in August 1861. Adam Cripps, a supplier of Civil War–era clothing for local privateer reenactors, provided period-looking garb for our reenactment team—replica schooner Captain Michael C. Murray, Steven C. Resler, and Matthew Armstrong. Without the assistance of LAMP, the St. Augustine Lighthouse & Museum, Captain Murray and his replica pilot schooner, the *Momentum*, the San Sebastian Winery and its wooden casks for cargo props, Adam Cripps's period clothing, and all the reenactors, these historical reenactment scenes for the *Jefferson Davis* privateer documentary simply would not have been possible (Figure 17.2). So, if you plan on shooting some historical reenactment scenes, seek out local historical societies, museums, reenactors, theater groups, and the local film commission, too, for assistance.

So, based on our experience, here are several suggestions for shooting historical reenactments:

1. If filming a reenactment of a battle scene, first check with the local law enforcement agency to make sure that discharging a replica weapon is permitted.

2. There are many types of reenactors, so be careful to choose the most authentic looking. There are some reenactors who spend lit-

Figure 17.2: Besides having good talent, documentary filmmakers need period-looking props to complement videotaping historical reenactments. During the production of *Search for the* Jefferson Davis: *Trader, Slaver, Raider*, the crew, with local assistance, found period-looking boats and wine casks for props (*credit: Peter Pepe/Pepe Productions*).

tle time or money trying to look the part. Then there are the more mainstream reenactors who generally look the part but who use modern conveniences after hours. Finally, there are the hardcore authentic reenactors who totally immerse themselves into their roles and the time period. These reenactors also usually own period eyewear and jewelry and actually groom themselves in period styles. The latter is what you want.

3. When the director and crew are shooting B-roll, as the archaeologist you should act as a technical advisor and be specific on what you want shot. Make sure the B-roll includes shots that are wide-angle, medium-range, and closeups. Make sure it also has the ambient noise of gun and cannon fire, if that was present.

4. Double- and triple-check all B-roll and other footage to ensure that it does not show anything with twenty-first-century hardware.

5. Finally, if the reenactment footage looks phony, then absolutely do not use it.

18
USING STILL PHOTOGRAPHY, HISTORIC FILM FOOTAGE, ILLUSTRATIONS, MAPS, HISTORIC NEWSPAPERS, AND ANIMATION

M AKING AN ARCHAEOLOGY-RELATED DOCUMENTARY has a unique set of challenges in that there is usually little in the way of film and video footage available that is pertinent to its historic people and events. We have already covered how reenactments can effectively re-create imagery depicting historic events. Now we examine how you can employ other mediums—photographic images, historic film footage, illustrations and paintings, maps, historic newspaper articles, and animation—to help present your documentary story.

Still Photography

Still photographs, whether old time or modern day, are frequently used by experienced documentary filmmakers. What can sometimes pose a problem, however, is a photograph's orientation, horizontal versus vertical. Movies, television programs, and documentaries are all horizontal formats, and thus it is difficult to use vertical images, since the aspect ratio is different. Vertical photographs can be utilized, but during postproduction, the editor may have to use only part of an image or create an insert, like a picture within a picture, which is essentially a small image inserted over the master shot, usually in an upper corner. If you

Documentary Filmmaking for Archaeologists, by Peter Pepe and Joseph W. Zarzynski, 127–132. © 2012 Left Coast Press, Inc. All rights reserved.

are giving the editor a CD or DVD full of photographs for possible inclusion in the documentary, it is best to make most of them horizontally oriented. The director or editor will specify how to present them, probably in high-resolution JPEG format of around 4 MB or more each.

As we noted earlier, a documentary is principally a visual medium supported by expressive audio. Therefore, visual action is important, even in still photographs. Award-winning documentarian Ken Burns, in his trademark eleven-hour-long 1990 PBS television production *The Civil War*, gave documentary filmmakers a lesson in how to create visual movement with still photographs. Because this documentary was about the Civil War (1861–1865), there was no film footage available, but there were black-and-white photographs. Fortunately, acclaimed Civil War photographer Mathew Brady (1822?–1896), working both independently and with a cadre of photographers under his direction, took thousands of photographs to visually document this horrific conflict (Morgan 2004). Born in Warren County, New York, Brady moved to nearby Saratoga Springs where, as a teenager, he met portrait artist William Page. Page introduced Brady to Samuel F. B. Morse, who had met photography innovator Louis-Jacques-Mandé Daguerre in Paris, France, in 1839, where Morse mastered his photography skills. Brady learned photography from Morse, and in 1844 opened a gallery in New York City (Figure 18.1). Many of Brady's Civil War photographs survived the war, and Congress later purchased them for $25,000. Today they are in the National Archives (Pritzker 1992:7–17). Ken Burns used these incredible photographs in his documentary and manipulated them during editing to give them movement, which is more appealing to the viewer than a static shot. This technique, known today as the "**Ken Burns effect**," consists of panning the photographs, moving from one subject to the next, and slowly **zooming** in and out on points of specific interest, kind of bouncing around to keep the audience's attention. Though Burns did not invent this editing technique, he is known to have perfected it—hence the name the "Ken Burns effect." Video editing software today has all sorts of panning and zooming effects that give movement to enliven photographs and other still imagery such as illustrations and paintings.

If you are a historic archaeologist, there are many repositories where photographs, illustrations, postcards, and maps can be found that might be suitable for incorporation into your documentary. Here is a

Figure 18.1: Mathew Brady was a nineteenth-century photographer whose crew visually documented the American Civil War (1861–1865). Historical photographs like those by Brady are sometimes utilized by documentarians in archaeology- and history related documentary productions (*credit: Mathew Brady/National Archives*).

list of a few archives and their websites to consult; note that the web addresses are subject to change without notice.

- Library of Congress (www.loc.gov/index.html)
- Smithsonian Institution (www.si.edu)
- New York Public Library (www.nypl.org/find-archival-materials)

Historic Film Footage

Other sources of images for archaeology- and history-related documentaries are historic films. One of the more popular archives for this type of footage is the Internet site Historic Films (www.historicfilms.com). This film archives is for professional use and charges a user fee to access its more than 50,000 hours of film footage of news events, entertainment, and music.

There are other film and video archives, too, including but not limited to the following. Again, note that the web addresses are subject to change without notice.

- NBC Universal Archives (www.nbcuniversalarchives.com)

- ABC News Video Source-NYC (www.abcnewsvsource.com)

- National Geographic Digital Motion, Washington, DC (www.ngdigitalmotion.com)

- Getty Images (www.gettyimages.com/Footage/Frontdoor/ArchiveFilms)

- HBO Archives (www.hboarchives.com)

- Absolutely Archives (www.absolutelyarchives.com)

Illustrations, Maps, and Other Historic Documents

Illustrations, paintings, and maps are also excellent visuals to enrich a documentary's story. If the production team decides to contract an artist to produce any drawings or painting to be inserted into the documentary, make sure the artist uses an aspect ratio that is the width-to-height ratio of the screen most likely to be used for your production—in most cases 16:9.

Historic maps and maps created using Photoshop and other software are often incorporated into archaeology and history documentaries. Some viewers may not be well versed in geography, so showing maps brings a geographic awareness to places mentioned in the documentary. The Library of Congress has one of the largest archives in the world for historic maps (www.loc.gov/rr/geogmap/gmpage.html). Another source for historic maps is the National Archives (www.archives.gov/research/start/by-format.html#cartographic). Both the Library of Congress and the National Archives are wonderful sources for cartographic information that is in the public domain.

Another place to search for illustrations and other images is the Gutenberg Project website (www.gutenberg.org/). Founded by Michael S. Hart, who passed away in 2011, the Gutenberg Project now has available nearly 40,000 e-books that are copyright free in the United States. There are many illustrations in these books that might be suitable for a documentary production.

Sometimes images of old newspaper headings make very effective visuals, if these can be acquired in high resolution. However, you will need to investigate copyright and the issue of **fair use** to see if you can use specific newspaper headlines. As a general rule, it is always prudent to get formal permission to use whatever images and quotes you plan to incorporate in your documentary unless they are in the public domain.

Animation

Finally, an imagery technique used by both documentarians and movie filmmakers that has certainly seen a rapid rise in its application is computer-generated animation. What is animation? Simply put, it is a rapid display of a sequence of images that creates the illusion of motion.

We can thank Winsor McCay (1867–1934) for his major contribution to the development of the animated cartoon, a forerunner of today's computer animation (Canemaker 1987:21). McCay was one of the most beloved comic strip illustrators of the early twentieth century, and for years he worked for newspaper tycoon William Randolph Hearst (Canemaker 1987:15–17). McCay did not invent either the comic strip or the animated cartoon genre, but his years of labor in both fields helped develop and popularize these art forms. McCay was introduced to early animation through **flip books**, which had been around for a few years. Flip books contained a series of drawings that varied very slightly from one page to the next so that when the pages were turned (or flipped) quickly, the figures on the pages appeared to be moving, or animated. Several years after McCay became involved in early cartoon animation, he released a short animated film entitled *The Sinking of the* Lusitania (1918), composed of several thousand images painted onto clear celluloid called "cels" and then registered over opaque backgrounds. This animated short, which also incorporated titles accompanied by dramatic music to set the mood of the wartime disaster, was a milestone in film. Not only was the animation a tour de force, but the production came out a mere three years after the *Lusitania* itself was torpedoed, so the disaster was still fresh in the minds of the audience when the film was released in 1918, which made it all the more memorable (IMDb 2012h). McCay's legendary film has been restored, and it can be viewed on YouTube; for anyone fascinated with early animation it is certainly worth watching. Years after McCay thrilled the public with his early animation success, another animation innovator, Walt Disney (1901–1966), enhanced early hand-painted animation techniques. Today, computer animation is quite common (IMDb 2012i).

There are many different types of 2-D and 3-D computer animation techniques and styles, from graphic animation to photorealistic and beyond. It is best for the archaeologist to discuss with the director the possible use of animation, its cost, and potential application. Creating effective animation takes a high degree of skill, and therefore this type of work is generally costly. Be advised that a few seconds of 3-D animation can cost several thousand dollars and can break a documentary budget. Nevertheless, your director probably knows some animators, and animation can enhance any archaeology documentary if it is based on the archaeological record and is well produced.

19
POSTPRODUCTION
AND EDITING

A FTER ALL THE FILM OR VIDEO SHOOTING HAS BEEN COMPLETED, it is time to move into the postproduction phase of the documentary project. This is an exciting time since it is the building or construction stage for the documentary. It is also when there may be a bit of a change in the day-to-day direction of the project. The director is still the creative boss of the production, but a new person now comes aboard—the editor. In small productions, of course, the director might have to do the actual editing, but in big-budget documentary productions, a dedicated editor assumes control of the editing while the director moves into the background to supervise and provide oversight. In this chapter, we offer insight into postproduction so that the archaeologist is cognizant of what happens during this very creative phase of documentary filmmaking.

Prior to postproduction, a lot of preparation has already been undertaken to make it easier for the editor to do his or her job. The footage shot during production may have been reviewed and logged (see Chapter 14), but possibly this remains to be done in postproduction. In some cases, footage deemed unworthy for inclusion into the documentary may not have been clipped. A log of the footage has been maintained that describes each interview sound bite and all the B-roll. The director has probably worked with the project archaeologist to gather all the archaeology-related graphics and photographs, and has possibly noted what animation, if any, needs to be produced. The editing script probably has been finalized or is close to completion.

Documentary Filmmaking for Archaeologists, by Peter Pepe and Joseph W. Zarzynski, 133–140. © 2012 Left Coast Press, Inc. All rights reserved.

Digital Nonlinear Editing Software

As the archaeologist on a documentary project, most likely you will not be tasked with doing the actual professional editing of the production. Nonetheless, it is important that you have at least an elementary understanding of digital nonlinear editing and software. Not so long ago, the postproduction process for editing video was more or less a linear process, in that the editor would start at the beginning of the movie or documentary and work in a linear fashion to complete the project in much the same sequence that the viewer would watch it, from the beginning to the end. All of that changed with the advent of digital nonlinear editing software. This has opened the door to a wide array of possibilities for the editor, not only from the standpoint of beginning wherever he or she would like, but also allowing modifications to the production wherever and whenever necessary. This has permitted editors to complete the production and then go back and "tweak" specific areas anywhere in the timeline.

A number of software products have become well established for the professional editor—for example, AVID, Apple's Final Cut, and Adobe Premiere, among many others. Pepe Productions has tried a few major brands and all work very well.

In recent years, software companies have marketed digital editing software "bundles." These are groups of associated software put together in a package or bundle that can be purchased less expensively than the individual applications sold separately. This is wonderful for selling software, but also great for people who want to teach themselves the full gamut of the art of film or video production, including audio, illustration, animation, and photo editing, in addition to video editing. If you are considering a purchase of a software bundle for video work, it is wise to familiarize yourself with the features and benefits of the different brands. Most of the popular software companies offer the option of a downloadable trial version so you can check it out before you buy. In most cases, these trial versions work just like the full-scale software but do not allow you to export your project until you actually make purchase the software. If you decide to buy, you can simply pay online; then you will receive a license and a pass code to activate the software to its full capabilities. There is no need to reinstall or start over.

Computers have become quite powerful, and their capabilities for helping to create quality video productions have brought creative freedom to many. However, keep in mind that the professional editor will always utilize computer hardware that is customized for optimum performance because that is what's required to process the complex graphics that have become the mainstay of today's editing styles. With access to the right hardware and software, startling 2-D and 3-D computer animations, along with video transitions that captivate the viewer, are limited only by the imagination of the creator. This, together with the fact that it no longer takes weeks or months to create these amazing effects, explains why video has become perhaps the most effective form of disseminating information, including archaeological knowledge, to the masses. We not only hear the story being told; we also see the details come to life before our very eyes.

Postproduction Phases

Though the postproduction phase of the project may differ in sequence of work from one documentary project to another, on most documentaries the same kind of work will be done in postproduction (see below). Let's take a look at these steps of the postproduction stage of documentary filmmaking.

Steps in the Postproduction Phase

1. **Assembly cut**

2. Rough cut

3. Narration

4. Music

5. Test screening

6. Fine cut

7. Finishing the documentary

1. Assembly Cut

The director and the camera crew have shot more video than will be used in your documentary—usually at least six to ten times more footage than the total number of minutes of the final documentary production. So, one of the earliest stages of editing an archaeology-related documentary is the assembly cut. After the footage has been logged, the director, editor, and most likely the project archaeologist will clip the production footage to get a feeling for the film. That is, the group evaluates the footage, keeps the best, tosses the bad, and sees how the good footage fits into the overall script. Somewhere along this process, the script is being tweaked, too, into an editing script.

2. Rough Cut

Next comes the rough cut, a polishing of the assembly cut so that the documentary begins to look a bit more like the final production. Tough decisions need to be made here so that the production is not overloaded with material. You have undoubtedly heard the expression "less is better." That holds true in documentary filmmaking. Therefore, here the director and editor cut scenes, sometimes rewrite the script, shape the production, and perhaps take a major turn in the slant of the story arc. There are discussions, maybe even arguments, but this is expected. These debates are good for the final production. Also in the rough cut stage, a preliminary narration track may be recorded, sometimes using the director or editor as narrator. This narration, a preliminary version, is for use during initial editing and to give pace for the final narration, which will be recorded later by a professional.

3. Narration

Somewhere in postproduction, the final narration (also called "voiceover") is recorded. The director may wait until all the kinks in the rough cut have been worked out before getting the narrator to record narration and add that track into the production. Selecting a narrator is a major part of documentary filmmaking. The director must decide: Do we want a male or female voice? Do we want a person with a regional or foreign accent? Sometimes a celebrity may be hired to bring a recognizable voice to the production. Regardless of whether a director selects a celebrity or simply an experienced voice talent, narration sets a tone for the documentary. Occasionally in postproduction, the narrator may have to be called back to correct mispronounced words or re-record a section.

4. Music

Movie makers and authors Dale Newton and John Gaspard, in their book *Digital Filmmaking 101—An Essential Guide to Producing Low-Budget Movies*, assert that there are few things as integral to a motion picture as quality background music (Newton and Gaspard 2007:227). The same can be said for documentaries. Selecting the best and most suitable type of music can improve the documentary and, conversely, having the wrong kind of music can go a long way toward ruining a production.

Wall-to-wall music in a documentary is generally not advisable, except in nature programs, where the music is vital because it serves to help move the narrative along (Cutler 2006:299). Background music for documentaries is largely without vocals, particularly in the narrative sections, as vocals would clash with the dialogue. (Vocals may have a place during the beginning or end credits, though.)

Where does the music come from? Seldom does a documentarian have sufficient funding to commission an original background music score and then hire a band or orchestra to record it. And, of course, it is not acceptable to use copyrighted music without written permission; using copyrighted music is illegal, even though nonprofessionals making small videos for YouTube and other Internet sites too often do so. Your director and editor probably will likely have to select from what is called "production music"—that is, stock music that has been written and recorded for, and is owned by, music libraries. This music is professional and is employed all the time in documentaries and other film and video productions. Production music or **royalty-free music** is purchased, and the purchaser has license to use the music in television, movies, documentaries, and on radio, too. However, it is imperative that the purchaser thoroughly read the license to see what production uses are permitted and what restrictions there may be. This type of music could cost as little as a few hundred dollars for several pieces of music or as much as thousands of dollars. There are many online production music libraries. To find these, simply search the Internet using the words "production music" or "royalty-free music." You can even listen to a few seconds of each piece of music; these are normally categorized by mood, emotion, or style, such as inspirational, classical, jazz, mysterious, solemn, military, and the like.

5. Test Screening

Somewhere in the postproduction phase, the director may invite key people for one or more **test screenings** of the rough cut or of various states of the postproduction editing. Test screenings are designed to elicit feedback, find problems, proof content, and aid in moving the production along to its completion. These screenings are invaluable to the director. Sometimes it is wise to hold several test screenings in order to hear from a balanced cross-section of people with varied perspectives. You might even talk the director into doing a test screening for your archaeological field crew or archaeology class. If the director is prudent, he or she will ask test screeners to complete a questionnaire and will even supply paper and pens so that people can jot down notes. It is also advisable to watch the audience in order to gauge their reactions to the documentary (Capon 2006:357). Following a test screening, the director or another principal acting as host can lead a discussion, asking for feedback on positive and negative parts of the production. It is important to foster an atmosphere that is conducive to getting honest and sincere feedback from the audience (Bernard 2011:195–197). Here is an opportunity, too, for the archaeologist to provide constructive criticism to the director and producer.

6. Fine Cut

The term **fine cut** denotes the final assemblage of the audio and visual components of a documentary or movie. Following the test screening of a rough cut, the director, editor, and archaeologist may have to go back to the proverbial "drawing board" and make changes based on test screening feedback. This is the final chance to also do another fact check to ensure that everything in the production is accurate, that the narration has no mispronunciations, that the opening and ending are exceptional, and that there are no audio or video blips. Some music may have been inserted during the rough cut stage, so the music is finalized during the fine cut stage of postproduction.

7. Finishing the Documentary

Once the edited interviews, B-roll, photographs and other still images, animation, narration, music, and sounds have all been inserted into the production, it is time to create explanatory annotations onto the screen and prepare and insert titles and credits.

Putting the titles and credits together presents a new challenge: this is where your editing team decides on font styles, prepares the list of credits, and selects music to accompany the credits. The archaeologist will be asked to come up with a list of key people involved in the archaeological elements incorporated in the documentary production. Hopefully, the archaeologist has been keeping a detailed and inclusive list and does not have to rely on memory to recall the names and jobs of key personnel. The credits section should not be taken lightly. These people are your colleagues, and they need to be given credit for their labor and assistance. Possibly the editor will ask for your input about titles and credits. If so, your simple and direct response should be that they are legible. That is, titles and credits should use a clean font and should be large enough to be easily read by all viewers. Also, ask the editor to leave the titles and credits on screen long enough to be read (Rosenthal 2007: 264–265).

The introductory credits, those listed at the opening sequence of the documentary, are brief and generally run for about 20 to 60 seconds. These may include the documentary title and the names of the executive producer, producer, director, and scriptwriter (Lindenmuth 2010:118).

Here is a suggested order for end credits for the major members of the documentary crew and those who assisted in the production:

- Title (optional)

- Executive Producer

- Producer

- Director

- Scriptwriter

- Editor

- Animator

- Technical Consultants (this would include the Project Archaeologist)

- Crew

- Archaeology Research Team Members

- Stock Footage, Photographs, and Other Illustrations
- "Special Thanks"
- Contact Information
- Suggested Books or Documentaries
- Copyright

This list will help the archaeologist and production assistant in compiling the all-important and all-inclusive credits list for the production. Do not forget to list (under the category of Crew, or "Special Thanks") the caterer, drivers, government agencies and municipalities that issued permits and permissions, marinas (if used), plane or helicopter company used for aerial footage, those responsible for providing the locales for interviews, and so on. Be sure to triple-check the spelling of all names and titles before committing them to permanence. It is quite embarrassing to misspell the name of a person or organization in the credits after they have dedicated time, effort, and talent to your production.

Following the insertion of descriptive annotations, titles, and credits, if there is enough money in the budget, the producer and director may decide to send the documentary out for video sweetening and sound sweetening. Video sweetening is a creative process that entails tweaking the video production's overall color, lighting, and balance to enhance the look of the visuals; generally this work is contracted to out-of-house professional video colorists. Sound sweetening is similar, but it is an audio fine-tuning to eliminate bad audio noise. If the documentary production looks good and sounds fine, then it can truly be said it was "professionally" created.

Finally, there may be another in-house screening of the documentary to check out the titles and credits and any other aspects of the production that may need to be changed.

20
THOUGHTS ON THE BEGINNING
AND THE END OF
YOUR DOCUMENTARY FILM

A S WE'VE REITERATED, A DOCUMENTARY FILM is fundamentally a story with a beginning, a middle, and an end. While each part of this story-telling formula is important, it is perhaps a satisfactory ending that con-tributes the most to an entertaining documentary. So, we start this chapter by first reviewing story endings. Not all documentary endings can be tidy, but it is nonetheless imperative to attempt to conclude the production with some type of resolution (Bernard 2011:30–31).

First, the Ending

There are two basic types of endings for a documentary, a closed end-ing and an **open ending**. With a closed ending, by the end of the doc-umentary the audience knows exactly what has happened. Nothing is left in doubt, and the viewers have closure to the story. An open ending in a documentary is one in which there are still some lingering ques-tions that remain unanswered (Das 2007:30–31).

In most documentaries, the scriptwriter knows the ending ahead of time and often will draft the script with that ending in mind. How-ever, not all documentaries are so neat; a conclusive ending is not al-ways possible—after all, life is sometimes a roller coaster. So, before we review the ways to create an effective start for a documentary (one that includes a solid hook to grab the viewers), let's look at the ending of one of our documentaries.

Documentary authority Alan Rosenthal acknowledges that not all documentaries have a nice, neat conclusion (Rosenthal 2007:121). Our documentary *Search for the* Jefferson Davis—*Trader, Slaver, Raider* is one that has a bit of an open ending, yet its conclusion is still satisfactory to viewers, many of whom are armchair explorers who "participated" in this archaeological detective story through the lens of the documentary camera.

Search for the Jefferson Davis—*Trader, Slaver, Raider* relates the story of a brig, the *Jefferson Davis*, through its various careers as a commercial vessel, an illegal slaver, and then an infamous Confederate raider, leading up to the modern-day investigation by underwater archaeologists and forensic scientists to find the lost shipwreck. The documentary crew followed a group of scientists in their quest, and, as in many stories that deal with an ongoing investigation, the culmination of their work, finding the shipwreck, was not fully achieved. The documentary concluded with the researchers of St. Augustine's Lighthouse Archaeological Maritime Program (LAMP) realizing that the shipwreck site they were studying, and which they hoped would prove to be the rebel privateer, may not be that vessel. To date, no diagnostic artifact has been found at the shipwreck site, so LAMP's leadership cannot declare that the submerged site is indeed the Confederate privateer. As they say, the "jury is still out" on the identity of their mystery wreck. Nevertheless, the LAMP team, determined and even defiant, announced in the documentary that they would continue to look for the *Jefferson Davis,* as the shipwreck is far too important, both to the local populace and the nation, to abandon the quest. LAMP's director, underwater archaeologist Chuck Meide, was so sincere in his declaration that LAMP would continue its scientific pursuit to find the shipwreck that this ending did provide the audience with an adequate conclusion to the documentary and even set the stage for a follow-up documentary down the road.

Here is the text for the ending of *Search for the* Jefferson Davis: *Trader, Slaver, Raider.* You can judge for yourself:

(Chuck Meide—Director, LAMP): "We're the detectives that are going to put these clues together and come up with a scenario that seems to make sense for our vessel."

(Chuck Meide): "What we know right now is that we believe this vessel is a probably a medium-sized sailing vessel. . . . It has very interesting construction features. It's very robustly built. . . . This most likely was a sheathed vessel. This technology basically became widespread by the nineteenth century. We have saw marks on some of the hull timbers from a band saw. That technology did not exist before 1808. . . . Basically, we know the vessel could not have been built before 1808."

(Samuel Turner—Archaeological Director, LAMP): "In a nutshell, we can't say if it is the *Jefferson Davis*, but we can't say it's not the *Jefferson Davis*."

(Chuck Meide): "We have certainly always been interested in finding the *Jefferson Davis*. It goes without saying that this vessel is of utmost national importance and certainly important to the history of the oldest port in the U.S. . . . But if we decide that we do not think that this is the *Jefferson Davis,* we're certainly not going to quit and stop diving and stop our archaeological research program. This is a major shipwreck and we're very interested in looking for it. We have other targets out there that we've already identified. Any of them could prove to be this Holy Grail of St. Augustine shipwrecks."

(Peter Pepe—Narrator): The story for the *Jefferson Davis* shipwreck is the tale of a diverse people—seafaring merchants, displaced and enslaved Africans, and Americans in conflict with themselves. After the privateer *Jefferson Davis* wrecked in August 1861, some Northern newspapers erroneously reported that the Confederate president himself had unexpectedly died. For a moment, some Northerners were relieved that with President Davis's death, the Confederacy would crumble. Unfortunately, as more accurate details of the privateer's destruction surfaced, Northern optimism soon disappeared.

(Peter Pepe): The Confederacy's most successful privateer had sunk, victimized by strong winds off the "Nation's oldest port." The "winds of war" would continue for another three and a half years.

(Peter Pepe): The archaeological investigation in the ocean sands off St. Augustine, Florida, is in reality a quest to examine oneself. For embodied in this shipwreck—the *Jefferson Davis*—is a pursuit by dedicated scientists to uncover the past and in so doing, gain a greater understanding of the "melting pot" of people we call the United States of America.

(Chuck Meide): "We will continue doing survey and using all the high-tech equipment at our availability to do the best we can to solve this mystery. She's out there somewhere and we have the tools that will let us find her. . . . *The search will continue.*"

The Beginning

Once you, the archaeologist, working with a scriptwriter, have a general idea of your documentary's ending, it is time to tackle another critical part of the production—the beginning. The beginning must immediately capture the audience's attention, create curiosity, and draw the viewers into the documentary tale. In the beginning of the production, the documentarian introduces the subject and establishes the message around which the documentary is built. The scriptwriter defines the "problem," the "crisis," or the "issue" that is at the heart of the documentary. Thus, an energetic start is very important. Nonetheless, because today's digital technologies no longer require that the scenes be edited in linear fashion (that is, in sequential ordering), if the team is stuck on that "grab 'em" start, you can hold off until that moment of revelation hits the scriptwriter and a great beginning suddenly emerges.

Here are two examples of beginnings for a documentary. Both use what is called a "back-door opener," a method of immediately enlisting the audience as active viewers as soon as the "doc" begins by delaying the opening credits and the documentary title until after the opening scene. This successfully captivates the viewers and is dramatic, too.

Here is the text for our first example, the opening narration of *The Lost Radeau: North America's Oldest Intact Warship*. Read it and try to visualize our back-door opener to determine if this type of beginning might be applicable for your documentary.

Opening Scene—The Lost Radeau: North America's Oldest Intact Warship

(Mark L. Peckham—National Register Program Coordinator, New York State Office of Parks, Recreation and Historic Preservation): "This is a touchstone of our experience with the French and Indian War. We have very few resources that survived from the French and Indian War period, and this one is preserved and handed down to us three centuries later in pristine condition."

(Kathy Abbass—Underwater Archaeologist, Bateaux Below, Inc.): "The twenty years before the American Revolution were very significant in the ultimate development of North America and people. . . . [P]eople just are not as aware of that so the radeau is an interesting poster child for that, if you will."

(Russell Bellico—Historian, Bateaux Below, Inc.): "Just recognizing how old this is, how large it is, how intact it is. There's nothing else like this that you can see underwater."

(Vince Capone—Sonar Expert, Bateaux Below, Inc.): "People believe that time travel is impossible. I say it is. When you dive on the radeau, you're literally transported back in time over 200 years. You are looking at a vessel that is the only remaining example of that class of vessel in the world—totally intact like the day it sunk. There are no other examples of this warship in the world. None that are close to bringing us back to that time in history. This . . . this is a time machine. It is a time capsule. It is a one of a kind in the world."

(Kip Grant—Narrator): Lost for over two centuries, "North America's oldest intact warship" rested hidden and undisturbed in the depths of a cold mountain lake in present-day New York state. Then 232 years after the vessel sank, it was discovered, a well-preserved icon of the French and Indian War. Take a journey with us as we explore one of the most historic but little-known warships in American history—the 52-foot-long *Land Tortoise*, flagship of "The Sunken Fleet of 1758."

The back-door opener was so successful for *The Lost Radeau* that we also employed it a few years later for our second underwater archaeology documentary:

Opening Scene—Wooden Bones: The Sunken Fleet of 1758

(Joseph W. Zarzynski—Underwater Archaeologist, Bateaux Below, Inc.): "Archaeology is a glimpse into the past. It's a window so we can find out what happened back then."

(Russell P. Bellico—Author, *Sails and Steam in the Mountains*): "Here we have the largest force ever assembled in North America—15,000 men. This armada stretched for almost six miles on Lake George, virtually covering the entire surface of the lake."

(Terry Crandall—Archaeological Diver): "I often thought about the actual character of the men that manned these vessels. What they did required almost super-human strength."

(Steven C. Resler—Coastal Resources Specialist): "The movement of goods, the movement of people, was all done on the water. It was all waterborne in the early days. So, that's where our beginnings are, that's where our histories began in this country."

(Mark L. Peckham—New York State National Register Program Coordinator): "Shipwrecks become time capsules of our historic experience. The environmental process may degrade them, but those are artifacts that are left as they were at the time they sank."

(Bob Benway—Underwater Photographer/Videographer, Bateaux Below, Inc.): "The historical record mentions that hundreds of these vessels were sunk in Lake George, but they never did say exactly how it was accomplished. So, what we see today instead of an entire boat is basically the flat bottom boards, the cleats, and the small nubs of the remaining frames."

(David J. Decker, P.E.—Director, Lake George Watershed Coalition): "When we talk about preserving and protecting the lake, it is important for us to recognize that it's not only the water quality that is necessary to protect, but it's also the historical significance of the area. Because the two go hand in hand."

Finally, the Middle

Now we get to the middle of the documentary. A cardinal rule for this part is "less is better than more." Some documentarians get lost in the middle of their documentary. Too many details can drag the production out and bore the audience. So, leave out unnecessary scenes or information. One option is to put this "unnecessary" but interesting information into **bonus selections** on the DVD to complement the feature documentary. Most viewers enjoy watching a "Deleted Scenes" section, and a streamlined feature documentary is superior to one that is drawn out with superfluous content.

21
THE DIGITAL REVOLUTION AND ITS ROLE IN DOCUMENTARY FILMMAKING

THE SO-CALLED DIGITAL REVOLUTION, moving from analog technology to digital, has been occurring over the past few decades and continues apace. It has created a rising wave in the number of documentary filmmakers, both professional and amateur. **Digital media** (or **new media**) are audio, photo, and video data that are electronically stored—that is, on computers and digital storage media—and digitally compressed. This development has democratized documentary filmmaking, as production equipment is now readily available at reasonable costs at chain stores like Best Buy and Radio Shack, as well as at retail outlets for Apple and other hardware manufacturers. So, rather than shoot a documentary on expensive film, as was done in the past, most documentarians today record visual and audio data onto digital videotapes, hard drives, and other digital recording media.

"Digital technology" refers to the method of recording information and encoding it. Digital technology operates on a binary system where patterns are assigned zeros and ones. Analog recordings, however, use infinitely variable patterns. Whereas digital recording can be reproduced at the same quality for each generation of an image and/or sound, analog recordings will deteriorate significantly from generational loss (Furniss 2008:286). This transfer of technology to digital media in the making of documentaries, television programs, and movies

Documentary Filmmaking for Archaeologists, by Peter Pepe and Joseph W. Zarzynski, 147–150. © 2012 Left Coast Press, Inc. All rights reserved.

started with major broadcast companies, but its more recent impetus came from the bottom up with small-time documentarians and film-makers embracing digital media due to its cost effectiveness, ease of operation, and growing availability.

Listed below is a chronology of the innovations that led the transition from analog to digital technology, thus promoting a new impetus in filmmaking and video production (Wallace 2012; Bellis 2012):

- 1970: CBS and Memorex designed the first digital, disc-based, nonlinear editing system, called CMX600.

- 1989: Avid released an off-line, nonlinear editing (NLE) system called Media Composer at a cost of $130,000; it revolutionized video and film editing, moving from linear to nonlinear editing.

- 1991: Kodak released the digital camera system (DCS), for professional photojournalists using a Nikon F-3 camera with a Kodak 1.3 megapixel sensor.

- 1992: The World Wide Web was released for public use.

- 1995: The DVD (digital video disc) was invented.

- 1999: Panasonic introduced pro-consumer (also called "pro-sumer") video cameras onto the market; Apple launched Final Cut Pro, a nonlinear editing system targeted to the consumer market.

- 2004: Apple's Production Suite was released for nonlinear editing.

- 2005: YouTube.com was launched.

- 2005: Apple released Final Cut Studio editing software.

- 2006: The Blu-Ray Disc was released.

- 2006: Final Cut Pro Studio was released.

- 2007: Apple released iPhone.

- 2010: Apple released iPad.

So, how does digital technology impact archaeologists who wish to get involved in today's documentary filmmaking industry? Think back a few years ago when archaeologists and archivists debated what type of photography to use for primary documentation of terrestrial excavations, submerged cultural resource sites, and artifacts. A couple of decades ago, the accepted norm in the field of archaeology was to use 35mm black-and-white film photography, as this provided the best quality for long-term archival preservation of photographs. However, as black-and-white and color film (photographs and slides) became harder to acquire (as they were being phased out by the digital revolution), digital photography, once considered suitable solely for secondary documentation, became much more accepted by rank-and-file archaeologists and archivists.

The technological transition that occurred in archaeology over the past two to three decades also took place in documentary filmmaking. Major television productions and low-budget documentaries and movies are now shot on digital video, assembled using nonlinear editing, and released in some type of digital format. This proliferation of digital media use by the younger generation is so omnipresent that the term **"digital natives"** is a popular description for those people born in the digital age. This same term can be applied to older people who were born in the analog era but who have wholeheartedly embraced digital technology.

Today's archaeologists have a variety of new media at their disposal to aid in documentary-style productions for Internet dissemination, DVD home video release, websites, and mini-documentary productions for museum and historical society exhibitions. The digital revolution has also made it much easier to gather information on documentary production and to promote one's documentary, too.

Social media groups such as the professional networking site LinkedIn can be harnessed to generate discussion among documentarians on various issues and concerns associated with their industry. Archaeologists can assimilate into such groups to gain quick access to professional advice on topics associated with documentaries. These groups are especially useful for getting valuable feedback from peers about projects in progress, and can also help archaeologists to network with film and video specialists for collaborative projects or to find a specific talent in your area of need. Other social media sites such as Facebook and Twitter are great venues for updating friends and associates about the progress of an archaeology-related documentary. Even as this book is being written, new innovative programs associated with the digital revolution will make understanding the process of documentary filmmaking that much easier for user groups of archaeologists, anthropologists, historians, and other social scientists.

So, rejoice! The digital revolution will continue to release new avenues to aid in the production of documentaries and in promoting them as well.

22
TELEVISION, THEATRICAL RELEASE, FINDING A DISTRIBUTOR, SELF-DISTRIBUTION, AND OTHER OUTLETS

W E HAVE OFTEN COMMENTED TO WORKSHOP participants and public lecture audiences that making a documentary is not overly difficult if you team up with talented and experienced documentarians. What may be daunting, however, is finding the best outlet for one's documentary release that will maximize the number of viewers and also generate enough money to pay off the production costs. Hard work is simply not enough to make a successful documentary program. There is stiff competition in the field. You need a fresh and terrific story with dynamic characters. You also require some timely luck. In this chapter, we guide you through some of the options for releasing your documentary production.

Television

Most archaeologists who dream of making a documentary about one of their archaeology projects probably envision that program being broadcast on a leading television channel. In Chapter 5, we reviewed some of those channels and their programs, and we list some of them again on page 152. Be advised, however, that it is extremely rare for a production company that works with big-time TV channels to ap-

Documentary Filmmaking for Archaeologists, by Peter Pepe and Joseph W. Zarzynski, 151–158. © 2012 Left Coast Press, Inc. All rights reserved.

proach an archaeologist they've not worked with before to undertake a documentary program. And, it is equally challenging to find an independent documentary filmmaker to team up with to create a documentary for one of these television channels. Nonetheless, as this book has provided you with a primer on documentary filmmaking for archaeologists and has offered insight on how to pursue your documentary dreams, we don't want to discourage you completely!

Here are a few of the television channels you may decide to contact to make a program proposal. Each has its own protocol for receiving a documentary proposal, so make sure your team is very familiar with the one(s) you wish to approach. Study their websites and television programs to determine if any of these channels are for you. It is your responsibility to determine what protocol is to be followed for documentary program proposals. Again, note that these web addresses are subject to change without notice:

- Discovery Communications: www.producers.discovery.com

- National Geographic Channel: www.natgeotv.com

- Public Broadcasting Service: www.pbs.org/producing/proposal

Theatrical Release

Nowadays, it is nearly impossible to get a documentary shown in mainstream movie theaters to be seen by Jane Q. and John Q. Public—unless your documentary has won a major film festival like Sundance or Cannes or garnered a major industry award. Then it will likely get picked up for nationwide distribution in theaters and, from there, a fast track to signing with a national distributor for cable television release, home video release, Netflix, and other venues. Later in the book (Chapter 23), we will review film festivals, what they are, and their critical importance to documentarians and filmmakers.

However, if you have a strong desire for a theatrical release for your documentary, you may be able to find an independent movie theater and negotiate a deal with the owner. In many cases, the independent theater proprietor may have several small theaters in your area, and this could broaden the local viewing potential, a crucial base to propel your production to financial success. There are plenty of community motion picture houses around the country; it's possible there are some in your geographical area. Many of these non-chain movie houses prefer to show independent productions, as these attract a certain clientele that prefers eclectic documentaries and movies. Archaeology-related documentaries tend to fit into that mold. Also, documentaries made by local documentarians are extremely popular, as local folks generally support hometown projects and productions. Thus, you have an excellent chance of persuading the theater owner that your documentary is worthy of several screenings and may even develop a cult-like following around the general community. This is a win-win situation. So, seek out those area theaters and inquire if they will screen your documentary. The local media, newspaper, radio, and television, would certainly wish to cover a story like that, too.

Finding a Distributor

Finding a distributor for your DVD documentary can be problematic. If successful, though, this will go a long way toward paying for production costs and making money for the documentary principals. However, there are some things to beware of when dealing with distributors. Some distributors will want to have all distribution rights assigned to them. Rather than accept this, consider splitting the rights. Your documentary can be marketed in many venues: DVD sales, video on demand, educational sales, website sales, and museum sales, among others. You probably will want to keep some of your distribution rights, such as website sales and theatrical sale rights.

Distributors look for documentaries that will generate profit, stir up some buzz because of media coverage or because of celebrities included in the production, that have won some awards, and that will "have legs"—that is, can sustain popularity for several years because the documentary is a "classic" (Capon 2006:354).

As we noted before, not all documentaries will be aired on television or will get theatrical distribution. So finding a distributor for home video release and other outlets is a big deal. However, there are a couple of advantages to DVD distribution that distributors, like the viewing public, recognize:

1. A DVD allows for anytime access by the audience.

2. Unlike documentaries that are viewed on television or in a theater, DVDs can include bonus selections. Informative scenes that were cut from the documentary can be refashioned and utilized to optimize the audience's viewing experience. Bonus selections can also be about the making of the documentary or can show interviews with the director, scriptwriter, and others, and can include additional intriguing shorts.

Distributors like to see bonus selections added onto a DVD documentary. These serve to complement the documentary feature. If the documentary is a few years old, adding a bonus section is an ideal way to update the documentary and make the DVD more appealing to the public (Capon 2006:354–355).

Here are a few of the many documentary distributors. Note that the web addresses are subject to change without notice.

- IFC Films (www.ifcfilms.com)
- New Video Group (www.newvideo.com)
- Documentary Educational Resources (www.der.org)
- Bullfrog Films (www.bullfrogfilms.com)
- Icarus Films (http://icarusfilms.com)
- The Archaeology Channel (http://www.archaeologychannel.org)

Netflix

Netflix is a subscription-based rental service that delivers movies, documentaries, and television shows on DVD, Blu-ray, and Internet streaming. The California-based company has been in existence since 1997. Contact Netflix to see if your documentary is eligible to be carried by Netflix (www.netflix.com).

Self-Distribution

If you totally strike out in your quest to find a national or regional distributor, then self-distribution for home video release may be the best avenue for you to pursue. However, you should be aware that the effort required for self-distribution is almost a full-time job. There are several things that you must consider. Your production team will need to design an eye-catching DVD disc cover, DVD box, and documentary poster (Figure 22.1). You may have to get this work done by a graphic designer who knows the industry standards for creating the DVD disc cover and the DVD box (Newton and Gaspard 2007:255-260)—things such as the NTSC Standard, aspect ratio of 16:9, DVD video logo, and the universal bar code, among others.

At some point, you will need to send out your DVD to be replicated and packaged. Before we discuss DVD replication, we need to mention that, as this book is being written (2012), digital media like CDs and DVDs are gradually becoming less prevalent, as downloadable files are ending up in the digital **cloud**. Music downloads have now surpassed CD purchases. For home video viewing in American households, digital sales, video on demand, and streaming have recently made monumental increases relative to DVD and Blu-ray sales and rentals. Book publishing is also moving into e-books rather than traditional printed and bound tomes, and audiences for watching movies and television shows via streaming technology have grown immensely, too (della Cava 2012:A1). Yes, the so-called virtual warehouse-in-the-cloud is rather busy. Certainly, if our book is fortunate enough to go into a second edition, we will most assuredly be updating readers on the newest developments about the digital cloud in documentary filmmaking.

Now it is appropriate to review how DVDs, a popular medium for viewing documentaries and movies, are created. Replication (as opposed to duplication) is the preferred method used to produce mass quantities of discs. In this process, a "glass master" of your original DVD-R or DLT (digital linear tape) is made and used to "stamp" the data onto a new disc during manufacture. A "clean room" environment must be maintained for proper "mastering" because the slightest piece of lint, dirt, or dust can create a defect that the master will carry over to the stamped copies. The disc is then printed and lacquered for protection. Replication takes longer than duplication because of the added steps in this process. Replicated DVDs can hold more information than duplicated DVDs, and they are less expensive per unit (given sufficient quantity). The biggest benefit of replication versus duplication is that a replicated disc will work on all DVD players and computer drives, whereas a duplicated disc works only on players that will read a DVD-R disc, which may preclude viewing on older DVD players.

As the replication of DVDs is being executed, the production team will decide on a retail price for the archaeology documentary DVD. The retail price should be neither too high nor too low. Do not be misled or influenced by the low cost of movie DVDs you see in some chain stores. These are motion pictures that have already had an extensive run in theaters, have probably been picked up and run by cable televi-

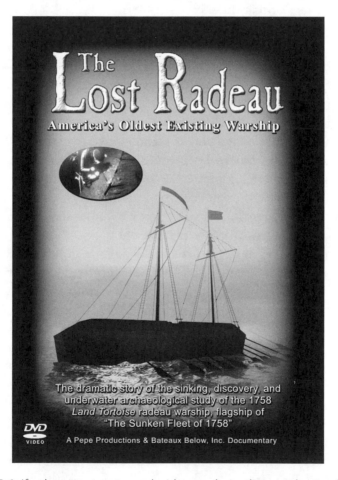

Figure 22.1: If a documentary team decides to release their production for home video, designing an arresting DVD case will help attract attention. Here is the DVD case for *The Lost Radeau: North America's Oldest Intact Warship*. Note that the DVD case design builds on some of the graphics from the documentary production's poster (see Figure 6.3) (*credit: John Whitesel/Pepe Productions & Bateaux Below, Inc.*).

sion, and now are out to make extra money from home video release. Thus, such DVDs are priced far lower than a first release. Your documentary will be on its first release and its price should be higher.

If you are working with an outside distributor, they will probably ask for a wholesale price of about 50–55 percent of retail: the distributor gets to keep 10–15 percent, and the retail stores they sell to get 40 percent. That means then the production group that made the documentary will receive only 45–50 percent of the retail price. So, factor that in when your team's leadership sets the retail price for the home video release DVD of your archaeology documentary.

If You Choose Self-Distribution:

1. Create a great website that promotes the documentary, as this is where the DVD can be sold via Internet orders.

2. Create an e-mail list of family, friends, business associates, professional and civic organizations, libraries, and schools that you believe might be interested in purchasing your documentary. Then send out news releases to everyone on your list. Make sure to cite your website to generate Internet sales.

3. Get your documentary into film festivals to promote your DVD.

4. Attend conferences, book fairs (yes, book fairs), and other events where you can sell your DVD. You should check first, but many book fairs do not prohibit sales of DVDs.

5. Send out news releases to newspapers, radio and television stations, blogs, and other media groups.

6. Contact local civic organizations and offer to give a presentation about your documentary. Most of the time, the civic groups are happy to have you to sell copies of the DVD after the talk.

7. Organize house parties and community screenings with large groups where you can screen your DVD and then sell it (Greenwald 2006:373). Some distributors, such as Bullfrog Films, will even coordinate community screenings for the films and documentaries they distribute.

As mentioned earlier, you will have to design and create a website to promote your DVD. The next chapter includes valuable information on this topic.

Important Advocacy Groups

There are several advocacy groups that support documentary filmmaking and documentarians. Here are some of these organizations. Again, note that the web addresses are subject to change without notice.

- International Documentary Association (www.documentary.org). Known as the IDA, this membership-driven, not-for-profit organization promotes documentaries and new media to foster public appreciation of the genre and the art itself. The organization offers seminars and other programs, publishes an informative magazine on documentaries and documentary filmmaking, and also hosts an annual awards event called the IDA Awards.

- Independent Filmmaker Project (www.ifp.org). The IFP is another membership-driven, not-for-profit corporation that advocates for the development, production, and promotion of both feature movies and documentaries. The IFP offers forums and symposiums, filmmaker labs, and other programs to help filmmakers and documentarians find funding for movies and documentaries. It also sponsors the Gotham Independent Film Awards and has other useful resources for its members.

- The Documentary Organization of Canada (www.docorg.ca). Known as DOC, this Canadian not-for-profit organization is a member-driven group that has chapters all around Canada. The DOC serves to promote, support, and help develop documentary filmmaking in Canada.

23
PROMOTING
YOUR DOCUMENTARY

PROMOTING THE PRODUCTION IS A HUGE ongoing endeavor for the principals of a documentary. However, before we get into marketing strategies—traditional publicity, Internet and social media dissemination, film festivals, and other ways to advertise your documentary—we start with some discussion about the look of the DVD's disc label, box, and poster.

Creating the Disc, Disc Box, and Documentary Poster

Toward the end of the documentary filmmaking process, the producer or director will most likely come to you, the archaeologist, to ask for your expert input into the design of the documentary's DVD disc label, box, and promotional poster. Even if your documentary will be distributed by downloads rather than via DVD, Internet-related promotion will still require a dynamic, creative graphic and image design to advertise your documentary. Therefore, it is essential that you find ample time to brainstorm with a designer to ensure a winning design for these. Just as a book's cover is one of the most crucial things a consumer peruses before deciding to purchase a book, so, too, is a documentary's "look" on the DVD's disc label, box, and documentary poster critical to its sale.

Documentary Filmmaking for Archaeologists, by Peter Pepe and Joseph W. Zarzynski, 159–174. © 2012 Left Coast Press, Inc. All rights reserved.

The graphic design for the DVD box needs to entice consumers as it communicates what the documentary is all about (Lindenmuth 2010: 135). In most cases, the producer and director will bring in a professional graphic artist, whether as part of the documentary team or as an outside contractor. But your suggestions, from an archaeological perspective, should be well received by the graphic designer. After all, some of the major demographic groups to be targeted for sales of your documentary will be archaeology students and professors, professional and avocational archaeologists, archaeological divers, cultural resource managers, and members of the public who are just plain interested in archaeology, anthropology, and history.

A documentary poster or movie poster is a very special part of your marketing efforts. The design should create enthusiasm through the use of poignant graphics and images. An excellent documentary poster will create "buzz" about the production—and good "buzz," by way of social media, print, television media, and word of mouth, is some of the best marketing you can hope to achieve. Your production team should not hold back on designing the poster. Seek the help of a professional graphic artist. Have the artist also create the DVD box cover using some of the same components as those in the poster so as to better **brand** your documentary's promotional look.

Besides the obvious—a short description of your documentary, the production company's name, and the length of the documentary—the cover of your DVD box should include these components, too:

- Title Logo: This should be prominently displayed on both the front and back panels of the case insert. Obviously, eye-catching graphics are necessary to draw attention to the package.

WOODEN BONES

THE SUNKEN FLEET OF 1758

- Universal Bar Code: Virtually all retailers who utilize computer-based systems for cash and inventory management will require that your DVD contain a bar code. These can be obtained from most replication companies for a nominal fee.

- The DVD video icon: The DVD video icon should also be displayed prominently, on the front, back, and spine of the box label. This is done to let the buyer know that they are purchasing a DVD video and not a CD-Video, Music CD, or other form of disc media.

- The world standard format icon: The world standard format icon for your DVD should be displayed on the back panel. As noted earlier, there are three main television standards used throughout the world: NTSC, the standard used throughout most of North America, by the United States and other countries whose television standard is 525 horizontal lines of display and 60 vertical lines; SECAM , which uses a 625-line vertical, 50-line horizontal display; and PAL (Phase Alternating Line), which uses a 625/50 line display. Because of these diferent technical standards, a video disc produced and replicated in the United States may not be compatible with equipment in other parts of the world without a standards conversion.

Your DVD disc has standards, too, for what should be labeled onto it:

- Copyright and year of release: It is also important to prominently display your copyright and year of release on the disc itself as well as on the back of the case insert of the DVD box.

- Title logo and DVD video icon: The disc face should also contain the title logo and DVD video icon.

Disc Protection and Security

Commercially produced DVDs are sometimes encrypted with region coding, Content Scramble System (CSS), and other artificial restrictions to keep the discs from being duplicated by unauthorized parties. A number of systems have been developed for this purpose. Unfortunately, there are also a number of free or low-cost software programs that allow the disc to be "ripped" or copied while bypassing copy protection encryption. This has been a bone of contention with movie and documentary producers for years, but it is always a sound idea to have your DVD encrypted during the replication process to protect against illegal pirating if you think your documentary will be widely distributed. Quite possibly, the best protection against **video pirating** is simply to register your work with the U.S. Copyright Office. This will allow you to bring legal action against anyone who may be unlawfully distributing pirated copies of your work.

Production Photographs

Besides having great still photographs depicting the various stages of your archaeological study, photographs of the production itself will be needed for publicity purposes. So, during the production of your documentary, request of the director that he or she have a professional photographer or a production assistant who is an accomplished photographer shoot plenty of production shots (Figure 23.1). Many times we have

Figure 23.1: Many times documentary crews are so busy they fail to get useful production photographs. Make sure you hire a professional photographer or use a production assistant to get quality production photographs such as this with documentarian Peter Pepe (*right*) and reenactors Brendan Burke (*left*) and James Bullock (*center*) during videotaping of a historical reenactment (*photo credit: Emily Jane Murray/Pete Productions*).

lamented that we failed to get good production photographs of the crew during the preproduction, production, and postproduction stages. You probably have run into the same predicament in the field during archaeological projects, wishing long after the fieldwork and lab studies were completed that you had more archaeological "action" photographs.

Check out our pointers (see below) for the documentary filmmaker or archaeologist who needs to get photographs for publicity purposes (Braun 2006:331).

Pointers for Getting
Good Action Photos for Publicity

1. If possible, hire a professional photographer to get production photographs of the crew when the team goes on location.

2. Make sure the photographer gets many photographs of the archaeology team in action, as well as of principals of the crew during the shoot of the documentary.

3. Ensure that the photographs are in high-resolution JPEG format.

4. Every photograph should be labeled with a title, date, names of the person(s) in the photograph, and a brief description.

5. Request that the photographer or production assistant get the proper releases signed for each person being photographed.

6. Get the photographer to sign over rights to the photographs in perpetuity so that your documentary team can use them wherever and whenever they choose.

7. Ask the photographer to shoot the images in horizontal format whenever possible and to shoot several photographs of each scene, group of people, or person using a wide shot, medium shot, and closeup shot.

Press Kits

A press kit, or media kit as it is sometimes called today, is basically an information packet about your documentary. Originally just a collection of informational handouts, graphics, and photographs, in today's new media world, press kits are also produced in digital format. That means a press kit will include the traditional packet of papers and photographs but will likewise include a CD or DVD with the same and, in most cases, added material, such as the documentary trailer and several video clips from the production (see list on facing page). The objective of the press kit is to grab the reader's attention, especially members of the press, and to answer questions the reader of the press kit is likely to have about the newly released documentary.

Film Festivals

Film festivals are an excellent venue for promoting documentaries. Unless your documentary was created for television release (in which case there is no need to enter it into film festivals), by entering film festivals your documentary and your production team can receive critical recognition and possibly even win awards. Just getting your film accepted into the festival usually confers the title "**Official Selection**" (Figure 23.2) —quite the promotional boon. There is another important reason to enter film festivals, too: Distribution companies often send their representatives there, and this could lead

Figure 23.2: Getting the coveted "Official Selection" into a film festival is a major goal for documentary filmmakers, as this will expose their documentary to the media and public. Here is a film festival "Official Selection" laurel for the 6th Annual Buffalo Niagara Film Festival held in the Buffalo, New York, area in 2012 (*credit: Bill Cowell/Buffalo Niagara Film Festival*).

Items for Your Press Kit

There are a variety of things that should go into your press kit (Magdael 2006:335–337):

1. An 8 ½ × 11 inch version of the documentary poster that includes the title, tagline, graphics, production company name, and contact and other relevant information.

2. A generic news release printed on the letterhead of the production company; this should include all of the above information plus a short summary of the documentary.

3. Up-to-date bios of the principals and major crewmembers involved in making the documentary. You should also include contact information (telephone number and e-mail) for some of these people so reporters can contact them for interviews.

4. Photographs of people in the documentary and production photographs.

5. Production notes, including why the documentary was made, when was it made, how long it took to make, where was it made, and a timeline of key events in the documentary and in the making of the production.

6. Media reviews, if any. Use only glowing media reviews.

7. A credits list of the major people involved in the documentary: the crew, consultants, etc.

8. FAQs (frequently asked questions).

9. Electronic Press Kit (EPK): As mentioned above, an EPK is a DVD with the following in digital format: production photo-graphs (JPEG format), photographs of the principals in the documentary, the documentary DVD box cover, the poster, pertinent graphics, the documentary trailer, several short video clips from the documentary, and other miscellaneous information.

10. Consider having review copies of the DVD documen-tary available to give to newspaper and magazine re-porters who may request them.

to your "doc" getting picked up by a national distributor (Lindenmuth 2010:128).

Film festivals are organized screenings of movies and documentaries that provide moviemakers and documentarians the opportunity to get their productions viewed by eager and supportive audiences and reviewed by professional critics. Getting your documentary accepted into a film festival can also generate newspaper, radio, television, and social media coverage. In addition, most film festivals bestow awards to filmmakers in a variety of categories, and some film festivals even give cash or product awards.

At no time in history have film festivals been so popular. There are hundreds of film festivals around the world that accept documentaries. Most film festivals show both movies and documentaries, and some film festivals—such as Silverdocs (Silver Spring, Maryland), the Hot Springs Documentary Film Festival (Hot Springs, Arkansas), Big Sky Documentary Film Festival (Missoula, Montana), Duke City Docfest (Albuquerque, New Mexico) (Figure 23.3), and Hot Docs (Toronto, Ontario, Canada)—are open only to documentaries.

To enter a film festival, usually you need a recently released documentary, one that is generally less than a year old, some money, and DVD copies of your documentary. Most of the time there is an entry fee, normally $25 to $100 or more. Quite often, the earlier you enter your documentary into a film festival, the lower the entry fee. As the final due date for submissions gets closer, film festivals will sometimes raise the entry fee.

The film festival's selection committee will require you to provide two or more copies of your documentary, probably in DVD format, to review and decide if it will be tapped as an Official Selection. In total, then, you will have to pay for the entry fee, the cost of the review DVDs, and the expenses for packaging and postage. Of course, just because you enter a film festival does not guarantee your documentary will become an Official Selection; competition is extremely intense, and there are far more documentaries being entered than there are openings in the festival.

The rewards of getting into a film festival are (1) you can use the film festival Official Selection for publicity, (2) you may win a film festival award, (3) it spawns news and social media banter, and (4) you might even get a distributor to select your documentary for distribution (Lindenmuth 2010:128).

Figure 23.3: There are numerous film festivals around the world, and a few are dedicated solely to documentaries. One such film festival is the Duke City Docfest held annually in Albuquerque, New Mexico (*credit: Jesse Quackenbush/Duke City Docfest*).

Today there is an organization called Withoutabox that serves as a central submission center for filmmakers to enter their productions for consideration into over 900 film festivals around the world. Owned by IMDb and Amazon, it also hosts video streaming on the Internet, strives to sell DVDs, and delivers video-on-demand downloads. To register to use Withoutabox, simply go to www.withoutabox.com.

Seeking Awards

Winning an award or honor for your documentary accomplishes two major things. First, it brings recognition to your "doc" and to the production crew, and second, it generates traditional publicity as well as new media coverage about the documentary award.

Most film festivals give awards, but there are also other avenues for seeking an award for your documentary, such as formal competitions. Here is a list of non-festival awards offered for documentaries. All have entry fees, so go the website of each awards entity and study their submission details. Do not wait too long after your documentary has been released or your production may no longer be eligible. Again, note that the web addresses are subject to change without notice.

- CINE Awards (www.cine.org)

- Telly Awards (www.tellyawards.com)

- Gotham Independent Film Awards (www.gotham.ifp.org)

- Aurora Awards (www.auroraawards.com)

- Peabody Awards (www.peabody.uga.edu)

- IDA Documentary Awards (www.documentary.org)

Traditional Marketing

We call this section of the chapter "Traditional Marketing" because this is old-school marketing that is still very effective.

News Releases

First and foremost, you should produce one or more press releases of various lengths about your documentary. These can be sent via e-mail and U.S. mail to local newspapers, magazines, radio and television stations, and special interest groups. Since your production is an archaeology-related documentary, you might also send press releases to regional schools, libraries, museums, and historical societies, as all of these organizations and institutions are likely to have an acquisitions budget to purchase DVDs about local archaeology and history.

Your news release should include the title of the documentary, a brief description of the documentary, its length, retail cost, how it can be purchased over the Internet, and where (in which stores and other locations) it can be purchased in person. If any local citizens were featured in, or participated in making, your documentary, be sure to include their names and a bit about what they contributed. You might even insert an informative quote about the production from the director or yourself. At the bottom of the news release, be sure to mention that photographs about the documentary are available, in digital format, on request.

Local Screenings

You should also consider hosting a special screening of the documentary for members of the media and VIPs, prior to its formal release. It is a smart idea to have food and drinks available at these screenings, as well as copies of the DVD for sale, and media members should be handed a press kit. Your team should make every effort to fill the theater or hall; if you have to, add your friends, relatives, colleagues, and acquaintances to the list of media invites. You do not want to hold a special screening designed for the media if you can expect only one or two members of the press to show up. Your screening hall should be jammed with people who will be positive about your documentary creation. Make sure you have documentary posters on display, too—you want this special screening to feel like a Hollywood gala. Some documentary producers go so far as to rent red carpets for the proverbial "red carpet entrance" associated with the Oscar and Emmy Awards ceremonies. Yes, in this case, "dress for success" also applies to promoting your documentary to the media and VIPs.

Postcards

Postcards that advertise your documentary might seem very old-school, but they are an absolute must. We may be in the digital age, but there is just something about promotional postcards that still appeals to us. Our documentary *Search for the* Jefferson Davis—*Trader, Slaver, Raider* was an Official Selection in the 2011 Orlando Film Festival (a truly filmmaker-friendly festival), the 2012 Amelia Island Film Festival, and the 2012 Buffalo Niagara Film Festival (Figure 23.4). We were surprised by how many film and documentary postcards were being distributed at their screenings, at after-screening parties, and at the awards ceremony. The participating filmmakers and documentarians were not bashful.

Movie and documentary postcards are traditionally a bit oversized, colorful, and bold. They list production company contact information and provide website and other social media direction. These are, in essence, oversized business cards. Relatively inexpensive to design and print, they can be inserted into press kits, handed out at film festivals and lecture presentations, and even mailed out. Models and actors have their promotional zed cards (also called composite cards, comp cards,

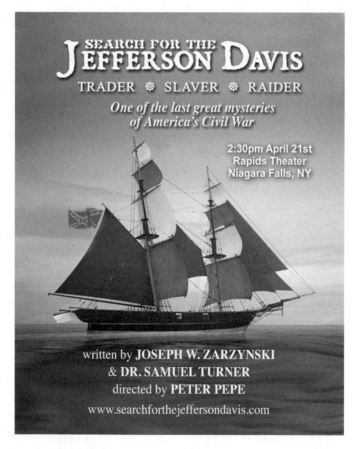

Figure 23.4: There are various avenues to pursue when promoting your documentary. One is to advertise your production. This catchy space ad, printed in the program for the 2012 Buffalo Niagara Film Festival, promoted the screening of the documentary in that event (*credit: John Whitesel & Peter Pepe/Pepe Productions*).

or z cards) that include multiple photographs of themselves, sort of a mini-portfolio. So, too, each documentary production team should use promotional postcards. The postcards can easily be designed and printed. Most important of all, they work!

Advertising

There is a common axiom in business, "You have to spend money to make money." That is true as well for marketing your documentary. So, set up a meeting with the producer to review the documentary production's advertising budget. At the meeting, define your audience's demographic area and then strategize how to optimize advertising funds to get the "most bang for the buck." You probably have a notion of which archaeology magazines to choose for space ads. Some documentary teams may even consult with market research companies to coordinate promotion and advertising. Provide the producer with a list of magazines, websites, and archaeology organizations that you believe will be intrigued by your documentary.

Building Your Website to Promote and Sell Your DVD Documentary

You should consider investing in a professionally designed website, not only to promote your documentary but to sell it, too, if you are doing self-distribution. Joseph Pepe, the Pepe Productions web designer and social media specialist, provided us with valuable tips when we were planning to get our website designed. A website for a DVD documentary might include a variety of things. Check our next sidebar for suggestions.

As mentioned previously, the documentary trailer is a mainstay for any documentary website. It should be prominent on the site and easy to find from the home page. An "auto-play" video on the home page is generally not a good idea: it can be startling and a turn-off to viewers. It is better to give viewers the option to press Play if they wish to watch the trailer. With today's technology that allows users to view video on mobile devices, it is essential that web videos are capable of being played on all platforms.

Items to Include in a Website for a DVD Documentary

1. The story behind the documentary—the "who, what, where, when, and how," including photographs and other illustrative graphics and images

2. Short bios of the cast and documentary production crew, including their photographs, especially production photographs

3. Easy payment options (if selling the DVD documentary through the website)

4. A section on awards and film festival information connected with the documentary

5. A trailer and other video clips available for viewing

6. A blog for periodic updates and viewer comments on the documentary

Keeping a blog is a relatively effortless way to update visitors on current news about your documentary. Announcements of where you are shooting, when your release date will be, when your trailer will be posted, where to find location photographs, and news about awards or film festivals are all appropriate blog topics. Blogs can also be used as a way to draw feedback and comments from viewers.

If you utilize a secure server for your website transactions, it can cost you a monthly fee, no matter how many sales you generate, plus credit card fees. The great thing about using PayPal is they do almost all the work for you. You designate your price for the DVD, shipping options, and sales tax, and they provide the code for you to paste into your blog or website. PayPal has no monthly fee and charges only when you transact a sale.

Another useful tool for all websites is a tracking system, such as Google Analytics. With some simple code that Google can create for you, you can periodically check your site's activity to see how many people visited, what pages visitors went to, how many people clicked onto more than one page, how long they spent on the site, and so on. This is useful information, as it may tell you if you should tweak your home page because visitors are departing the website quickly or if they are going right to the trailer and watching it.

The Internet and Social Media

The Internet and social media have opened new portals to boost interest in documentaries. Social media networks like Facebook, Twitter, and LinkedIn, as well as blogs and other emerging programs in this field all can help to foster interest in your documentary and create new customers for your product.

Social media have become practically mandatory for disseminating news of product launches, including movies and documentaries. Almost every Hollywood movie gets a Facebook page before its trailer is released, and the same should hold for documentaries. Social media websites allow fans and users to interact, be updated, stay current, and connected. Friends, colleagues, and relatives who share your interests or who may be looking forward to a video can click one button to stay current with news on your documentary. These sites, however, work in conjunction with your website and should not replace it.

The 2010 Academy Award–winning Best Documentary, *The Cove* (released 2009), about Japan's dolphin-hunting practices, has several hundred thousand "fans" who have "liked" their Facebook page, and thousands of Twitter followers, too. While the documentary is not a recent release, the production company's continuous updates on social media sites keep their fans current, and they also sustain a large audience for new information and future project promotions. It can take some time to build up a fan base on social media. It often starts with friends, family, and co-workers but can grow into other sections of society. The more interactions you have, the more successful you will be in building your audience—and it costs only the time it takes to write and post your updates. One sale of your DVD or one referral from your social media site can lead to a number of other word-of-mouth referrals.

Social networking is a growing phenomenon used by millions of people around the world to connect with others, start new relationships, and help promote programs and products. Get accustomed to using it!

The traditional and emerging promotional strategies covered in this chapter are all necessary to effectively promote your documentary and its archaeology project as well as to set the stage for future documentary production endeavors.

24
DOCUMENTARIES
IN MINIATURE

TODAY, THERE IS A GROWING TREND FOR ARCHAEOLOGY-RELATED documentaries that are shorter in length than the traditional feature-length documentaries customarily viewed in theaters, on television, and as home video and download releases. These abbreviated documentary-style productions are finding outlets on the Internet, in museum and historical societies, and elsewhere. This means there will be more venues for archaeology documentaries, which is indeed welcome news for archaeologists. So, we would be remiss if we did not examine this expansion of the documentary filmmaking arena into what we call "documentaries in miniature" or "mini-docs."

Museums

Increasingly, archaeology-, history-, art-, and nature-related documentaries are being made specifically for screening in museums and to accompany traveling exhibitions. Museums that have auditoriums are hosting feature-length documentaries. In 2012, the Museum of Florida History in Tallahassee screened our documentary *Search for the* Jefferson Davis—*Trader, Slaver, Raider.* At 50 minutes long, the video is somewhat lengthy for a museum program, but it complemented the Florida state museum's new exhibit entitled "Ships, Sailors, and Shipwrecks of Civil War Florida."

Documentary Filmmaking for Archaeologists, by Peter Pepe and Joseph W. Zarzynski, 175–180. © 2012 Left Coast Press, Inc. All rights reserved.

Though many well-established museums have state-of-the-art theaters for screening documentaries of any length, museums and historical and science institutions in the twenty-first century are drifting more toward mini-documentary productions that are fully integrated into exhibits. The advance of documentaries into museum exhibitions is thus an opportunity for documentary filmmakers and archaeologists to interface with museum exhibit planners. Museums provide a one-of-a-kind atmosphere for optimizing public outreach because they can combine traditional exhibit formats interwoven with digital media such as mini-documentaries, PowerPoint (PC and Mac) and Keynote (Mac only) presentations, and even 3-D projection programs. Whereas traditional documentaries bring the world of the archaeologist and anthropologist to the viewers, museums today can offer documentary-style productions combined with the display of **material culture**, thus giving museum patrons the opportunity to inspect the re-created world of the past. For museums, mini-docs need to work in conjunction with displays of artifacts, photographs, 2-D signage, and other items in the exhibit halls. This type of alliance of inserting short documentaries into traditional museum exhibits is likewise very suitable for traveling exhibitions that can go on the road for several years. Exhibit programs like this frequently have well-endowed corporate sponsorship, so documentarians and archaeologists would be remiss not to explore the museum option as a venue for documentary-style productions.

That said, documentarians, archaeologists, and technicians working on museum exhibits of this kind face some challenges not encountered in making standard-length documentaries on archaeology. Here are some of those points to consider when planning a documentary in miniature for museums (Krinsky 2011):

1. Documentary-style productions for museums have far less time to tell their story than television or standard-length documentaries. In fact, museum visitors touring an archaeology gallery will usually give you no more than three to four minutes of their attention per mini-documentary, about the maximum time that a person can comfortably stand to watch a video.

2. Mini-docs designed and produced for museums really need to draw the viewers in and involve them in the experience of museum visitation. Documentary productions for museums must

make their viewers connect with the artifacts on display and with the people who once used this material culture.

3. Because of the above two challenges, a lot of information and emotion need to go into a compressed period of time.

Training DVDs and Instruction

Documentary-style filmmaking is likewise quite appropriate for other nontraditional applications such as instructional or training DVDs and even for long-distance learning at institutions of higher learning. One person who realized this potential several years ago and who has created a niche market for his training DVD productions is Vincent J. Capone, president of Black Laser Learning. Capone, a nationally known authority on side-scan sonar and other marine remote sensing equipment, decided several years ago to specialize in developing and selling training DVDs as a teaching tool for his highly technical and specialized field.

Side-scan sonar is frequently used in oceanography, marine exploration, and underwater archaeology. It utilizes acoustic energy transmitted over the seafloor or lake bottom either from a towfish attached to a cable and generally towed from a survey vessel or as part of the equipment package on an autonomous underwater vehicle (AUV). This kind of sonar (which stands for sound navigation and ranging) is a superb piece of remote sensing equipment used for detecting shipwrecks and other submerged cultural resources (Klein 1997:384–385). However, it requires well-trained operators, and training facilities offering instruction are somewhat few and far between. Thus, Capone, who periodically travels around the country presenting workshops on side-scan sonar, realized the potential of employing video productions with expert instruction, informative animation, and illustrative video footage to train people in side-scan sonar's use and interpretation (Figure 24.1). Capone realized that rather than write another book or training manual on the subject, which he thought would be redundant, he should produce training videos. Thus, he discovered a practical method of teaching side-scan sonar—training DVDs—which had not been exploited previously. Some of his remote sensing training DVDs are *Not in the Manual: Guide to Side Scan Sonar and Magnetometer Surveys*, *Principles of SONAR & MAG for Underwater Archaeologists and Cultural Resource Managers*, and *Not in the Manual: Guide to Subbottom Profiler Surveys*.

Figure 24.1: 3-D artist/animator Ryan Knope works on animation for Black Laser Learning's remote sensing training DVDs. Documentary-style DVDs have been produced by Black Laser Learning to facilitate the training of people in the principles and operation of sophisticated side-scan sonar and autonomous underwater vehicles (*credit: Steve Tampa*).

Likewise, there is great potential in archaeology for a series of skillfully produced instructional DVDs targeted at university-trained archaeologists seeking additional professional development as well as for avocational archaeologists who desire training in various aspects of archaeology. We also see an as-yet untapped market for educational feature-length and mini-documentaries in the field of long-distance learning for colleges and universities. We are sure that this void will soon be filled by enterprising institutions of higher learning that want to provide their students with the best in instruction.

The YouTube Phenomenon and Internet Viewing

Moving outside the institutional walls into cyberspace, there is an incredible explosion of worldwide popularity in the YouTube phenomenon and other Internet viewing venues for short videos. You probably will not get paid for this type of production, but you can certainly find a viewing audience here. This cyberspace marvel has created previously untapped opportunities for both professional and amateur documentarians to get their creative efforts released to the public.

YouTube, at www.youtube.com, is the most well-known website for users to upload their videos for free Internet viewing. Based on the number of daily visits, it is one of the most popular websites in the world. YouTube has videos on every topic imaginable—including on archaeology and documentary filmmaking. Uploading a video to YouTube is not difficult. Google, the company that owns YouTube, has a website link to create and manage your account and get started: http://support.google.com/youtube/bin/topic.py?hl=en&topic=16546.

Furthermore, in 2012, YouTube announced plans to expand its programming by committing $100 million in seed money to support the production of well-funded and quality-content videos using some of Hollywood's best filmmakers (Nakashima 2012).

The advantages of posting a documentary trailer on YouTube for embedding in or linking to your website begin with it being hosted on the most widely used video-sharing site in the world. If you carefully choose the tags you place with your YouTube documentary trailer, you will automatically increase the hits to your site because more Internet searches will find it. Perhaps the greatest advantage of using YouTube is that every computer, no matter the operating system, will be able to view your video as long as the computer and its Internet connection will support online video. YouTube has a convenient compression and player system that allows near-immediate start of the video and progressive download, which means that once it starts to play, it should play through completely and uninterrupted. Of course, this again depends on one's computer Internet connection speed.

YouTube is not the only video hosting site. Others include Vimeo, AtomUploads, Blip.TV, BrightCode, and ClipShack, just to name a few. If you examine each website's capabilities, you will find that some, if not most, will allow you to create your own online TV channel which can include many of your own productions.

Mini-Videos on Websites

As an archaeologist, you have a professional responsibility to "publish" the results of your research and field investigations. Outlets for publication have long included "gray" literature (that is, cultural resource management reports), lectures and professional papers delivered at conferences, articles in professional journals, articles in popular magazines, and books released by traditional publishers. Today that list encompasses developing museum exhibits, striving to get your work covered in a documentary, creating informative websites, and utilizing social media networking.

Several years ago, it was enough to have a website that was well designed and included informative graphics, photographs, and text. Things have certainly changed, in part driven by the vast usage and success of the YouTube phenomenon. Today, outstanding websites have matured so that they generally include one or more short video productions and videos that are professionally created, too.

The key words here are "professionally created." Anyone today with an HD video camera, a computer, editing software, and some basic skills in videography can make a satisfactory video production. However, there is still nothing like using professional documentary filmmaking talent. Thus, to enhance your archaeology project, it would be wise to find the funds to hire professional documentarians. The results will far surpass an amateur production in showcasing your archaeology project and optimizing public outreach. One way to do this is to get several archaeologists together to pool their financial resources and hire a single professional documentarian team to create a series of mini-documentaries. The expression, first attributed to President John F. Kennedy, "a rising tide lifts all boats," certainly applies here. The more professional-looking your archaeology video production, the greater the status of social science in the eyes of the general public, business, and government. Everyday we see terrific high-quality video production on our television sets. Thus, as Americans we have come to expect to see that same quality, and nothing less, in the other videos we watch.

25
CREATING YOUR TRAILER

IN CHAPTERS 23 AND 24, WE MENTIONED THE IMPORTANCE of creating a documentary trailer, but we did not define what a trailer is, discuss the history of trailers, or explain what a documentary trailer should include. In this chapter we review these topics.

One of the most effective things a filmmaking team can do to promote their production is to make a trailer—that is, a short film or video preview whose purpose is to serve as an advertisement for a movie, documentary, or television program. Most documentary trailers are under 2.5 minutes (150 seconds), the time mandated for theatrical trailers by the **Motion Picture Association of America** (MPAA). However, in our world of "give me the information as fast as you can," the optimum time for a documentary trailer is probably about 90 to 120 seconds, less if it is for television. That said, you will find some trailers as long as three minutes or more.

Movie trailers are so popular with the public nowadays that some cable television networks offer movie trailers on demand. Naturally, though, trailers are easy to find on the Internet. If you want to indulge your taste for movie trailers, visit the website www.reelz.com. Two other excellent websites for viewing documentary and movie trailers are www.imdb.com and www.youtube.com.

The "trailer" got its name in the earlier days of motion picture viewing, when they were customarily shown after the feature film was screened—not before the feature movie, as is the case today. Because theater patrons didn't want to stick around after a feature length movie

Documentary Filmmaking for Archaeologists, by Peter Pepe and Joseph W. Zarzynski, 181–184. © 2012 Left Coast Press, Inc. All rights reserved.

was over, it quickly became standard practice to screen trailers before the feature as an advertisement for that movie or other movies. The name stuck in the filmmaking industry.

To confuse matters somewhat, there are some movie and documentary filmmakers who have different ideas about what a trailer is. They maintain that there are a variety of trailer types—trailers for fundraising, trailers that preview movies for audiences in theaters and elsewhere, trailers that serve as a teaser, and those that are done as a work sample (Rossi 2005:3–7). For our purposes in this book, we are calling a trailer a roughly 2.5-minute-long preview that gives basic information about the feature-length documentary. Under this definition, trailers are designed to persuade viewers to:

1. purchase a ticket to gain entry into a theater,

2. turn on one's television to watch a documentary,

3. buy the DVD documentary, or

4. download the documentary to watch the full feature on one's computer.

Many documentarians create several trailers, of varying lengths, for a single documentary, each version customized to fit the profile of the intended viewing group.

So, what content—images, audio, and text—should go into a documentary trailer? To get your audience to take one of the four actions noted above, first and foremost your trailer needs to pique the viewer's interest (Lindenmuth 2010:122). To do this, and to provide important information about the documentary, follow the guidelines in our list on the facing page. These show just how much material you have to squeeze into a trailer. In fact, making a successful trailer is a true art.

One other thing: Since we are talking about a trailer for a documentary, and since documentaries should strive to be truthful, your trailer must not be misleading (Lindenmuth 2010:122). In Hollywood, where big-time money fuels the motion picture industry, it is not surprising that there are production companies that specialize solely in creating film trailers. For the most part, these businesses have thoroughly mastered their craft. Unfortunately for viewers, sometimes a film trailer will be so mesmerizing that it persuades us to purchase a

A Trailer Should:

1. Introduce viewers to the documentary story and its conflict

2. Immediately grab the viewer's attention

3. Introduce the documentary's protagonist and antagonist

4. Briefly sum up the documentary without giving away the ending

5. Use the most exciting footage to intrigue viewers

6. Display the production company and distribution company's names near the beginning of trailer

7. Provide the title of the documentary near the beginning of the trailer

8. Show off some appealing cinematography

9. Use great music and change the background music a few times over the course of the 2.5 minutes

10. At the end, include the title of the documentary, the principal cast and crew, the documentary trailer website, and any other contact information.

theater ticket or to buy, rent, or download the DVD or Blu-ray, only to leave us rather disappointed in the feature film.

There is even an Oscar- or Emmy-type competition for movie and documentary trailers, called the Golden Trailer Awards. It is well worth it to go to their website to get details on these awards and also to watch some award-winning trailers. If your documentary filmmaking team succeeds in fashioning a noteworthy trailer, ask the producer or director to consider entering it into the Golden Trailer Awards competition. As with most film and documentary awards competitions, there is an entry fee. For more information, go to www.goldentrailer.com.

In summary, the archaeologist on the team should work with the director and editor to produce a masterful trailer, one that persuades viewers of all ages to want to watch your archaeology documentary. If you succeed in creating that A+ trailer, it will assuredly draw throngs of people wishing to watch your feature production.

26
CONCLUSION

NOW THAT YOU HAVE FINISHED READING MOST OF THIS BOOK, we hope that you, the archaeologist, will be much better prepared to seek out and form that documentary filmmaking collaboration to meet your goal of seeing a documentary produced about your archaeology project. There is an adage that asserts: "Everyone has one good book in them." A corollary to that in the documentary filmmaking genre might be: "Every archaeologist has one good archaeology documentary in them." We happen to think that this is indeed true. There are many fascinating archaeology stories out there just waiting to be told by documentarians. So, do not wait for that documentarian to rap on your office door to invite you to become part of his or her team. That knock on your door or telephone call invitation just may never happen. As we mentioned early in the book, we believe that a documentary is simply a story waiting for its storyteller. Therefore, we urge you to seize the initiative and go out and find that eager documentarian, your future documentary collaborative partner. To borrow from the halls of Hollywood, the Sundance Kid needed to find Butch Cassidy and Louise was really not Louise until she allied herself with Thelma.

Noted author Malcolm Gladwell, in his best-selling book, *Outliers: The Story of Success* (2008), repeatedly refers to the "10,000-Hour Rule." Gladwell affirmed that an overriding reason for success in any occupation is primarily based on having 10,000 hours of experience in that particular field. Certainly there are also other factors involved in becoming a winner, consummate in your occupation, such as motivation and even a wee bit of luck. If Gladwell's philosophy has merit, as many of his readers wholeheartedly believe, then we hope this book, *Documentary Filmmaking for Archaeologists*, has been enlightening to you. Now that you have this background and newly gained insight into documentary filmmaking techniques, you have made significant strides, if not a quantum leap, toward reaching Gladwell's "10,000-Hour-Rule."

In today's rapidly changing world, the peoples, countries, and cultures that inhabit our planet have become interdependent. Therefore, the study of archaeology and disseminating the results of its investigations will give us greater cultural awareness. Knowing more about our collective past and being more culturally sensitive to those around us will bring us closer to the wisdom needed to make better decisions during the formidable challenges certain to await us. Documentary filmmaking is a critical informational tool for fostering our understanding of multicultural perspectives.

Therefore, we reiterate our favorite quote from our DVD production colleague, Vincent J. Capone (Black Laser Learning): *"A story is not a story until the story is told."* It is now time for you to take the next steps toward telling your archaeology-related story using the dynamic genre of documentary filmmaking. We know you can do it, and we cannot wait to see your archaeology documentary or television program. Good luck and let us know when your documentary premieres.

Appendix 1
SAMPLE
DOCUMENTARY PROPOSAL

"Search for the *Jefferson Davis*: Trader, Slaver, Raider" (Pepe Productions), February 2009

1. Documentary Film Title
Original working title: "The Forgotten Confederate Privateer: The Search for the *Jeff Davis*, A Civil War Raider"[1]

2. Documentary Statement
"Search for the *Jefferson Davis*: Trader, Slaver, Raider" is the documentary story about one of the most feared, yet little-known privateers of the Civil War (1861–1865), and the archaeological search to find the lost shipwreck. Pepe Productions, in conjunction with the St. Augustine Lighthouse & Museum in St. Augustine, Florida, and its maritime branch, the Lighthouse Archaeological Maritime Program (LAMP), will collaborate to produce a feature-length documentary.

3. Background on the Documentary's Topic and the Need for the Production
The project will be the first documentary film production to investigate one of the last great mysteries of the Civil War—where is the Confederate privateer, *Jefferson Davis*, an undiscovered shipwreck? The documentary will inform viewers about one of the most historic, but

Documentary Filmmaking for Archaeologists, by Peter Pepe and Joseph W. Zarzynski, 187–190. © 2012 Left Coast Press, Inc. All rights reserved.
[1] The title was eventually changed to *Search for the* Jefferson Davis: *Trader, Slaver, Raider*.

188 ■ Appendix 1

little-known shipwrecks lying off the "First Coast," the shores of St. Augustine, Florida. With the 150th anniversary of the Civil War less than two years away, April 12, 2011, this documentary will certainly be timely. Using the documentary approach of "the search," the production will tell the story of the *Jefferson Davis* (also known as the *Jeff Davis*), the first great Confederate privateer of the Civil War, as well as the history of the vessel before the Civil War began when the brig was a commercial vessel and then engaged in the illegal trans-Atlantic slave trade. Furthermore, this is the engaging story of a group of dedicated scientific sleuths who are using the principles of underwater archaeology to find a historical treasure. These researchers, members of the Lighthouse Archaeological Maritime Program (LAMP), St. Augustine Lighthouse & Museum's maritime heritage unit, will explore the waters off America's oldest city, hoping to discover one of the last icons of America's bloodiest war, a feared privateer with a black hull, black masts, and black sails. The DVD production, approximately 35 to 50 minutes in length, is being produced for home video release. The documentary will not only investigate a 150-year-old maritime mystery, it shall likewise inform viewers about underwater archaeology, thus promoting this social science.

4. Approach and Style

The documentary, to be shot in 16:9 aspect ratio wide-screen format, will begin with the LAMP team about to prepare for their archaeological search for the *Jefferson Davis* shipwreck, involving a summertime field school in 2009 designed to teach college students to be underwater archaeologists and also to possibly find the rebel raider. The documentary will then flash back to the mid-nineteenth century to tell the intriguing tale of the Baltimore-built sailing vessel when it was known as the *Putnam* and later named the *Echo*, before it became the famed Civil War marauder, *Jefferson Davis*. The documentary will then focus on the scientific search for the *Jeff Davis*, as the vessel was commonly known during the Civil War, as researchers work together to solve this archaeological jigsaw puzzle.

5. Audience

The audience for the documentary will be for the general public, but the production is sure to be popular for Civil War aficionados, history buffs, middle and high school students, local residents around St. Augustine, Florida, and those people wishing to be armchair investigators to "participate" in the search for this nearly forgotten Confederate privateer.

6. Budget

Pepe Productions will assume all production expenses, less travel costs, replication costs for the DVDs, and all major computer-generated animation and still images fees.[2]

7. Schedule

On-site documentary filming will begin June 2009 in St. Augustine, Florida, during LAMP's summer field school to test the hypothesis that one of the sunken vessels of a "double shipwreck" is the privateer *Jefferson Davis*. A shooting script will be in place prior to the June 2009 field shoot. Since this documentary uses "the search" format, a full script cannot be completed until after the video shooting. There is the possibility that one or more LAMP members will have to fly to Albany, New York, for a couple of days of pre-field school interviews with Pepe Productions (Glens Falls, New York) since the slant of the production is "the search." Following the Florida field shoot, Pepe Productions will need to go to Charleston, South Carolina, Baltimore, Maryland, and possibly other locations before going into the postproduction stage of the documentary to finish the editing script and begin editing.

8. Key Filmmaking Team, Brief "Bios"

Pepe Productions Documentary Production Crewmembers

Peter Pepe (director and chief cameraman): Peter Pepe has over 25 years of professional experience making video productions, with work in all facets of this industry.

Joseph W. Zarzynski (documentary co-scriptwriter, location manager): Joseph W. Zarzynski is an underwater archaeologist, has been a producer and a scriptwriter on two other underwater archaeology

---

[2] Generally, budgets included in a documentary proposal will give at least the final production fee and possibly even major itemized costs. A complete itemized budget will most likely be required during production negotiations between the documentary's principals and the commissioning agent.

documentaries made by Pepe Productions, and has traveled with Pepe Productions on corporate video fieldwork around the USA.

Steven C. Resler (underwater videographer): Steven C. Resler is a coastal resources specialist, veteran scuba diver, and underwater photographer and videographer.

John Whitesel (animator): John Whitesel is a nationally recognized computer animator with vast experience creating animation of sailing watercraft and shipwrecks. His animation has appeared in documentaries, museum and visitor center exhibitions, television commercials, and in other new media.

Production Assistant (to be determined)

LAMP Personnel

Kathy Fleming (Executive Director, St. Augustine Lighthouse & Museum)

Chuck Meide (Director, LAMP)

Samuel Turner (Archaeological Director, LAMP, and documentary co-scriptwriter)

Brendan Burke (Archaeologist/Logistical Coordinator, LAMP)

Christine Mavrick (Conservator, LAMP)

9. Miscellaneous

The documentary will be distributed through both retail and Internet sales and possibly through Internet downloads. At a later time, should the opportunity arise, the partners might wish to explore updating the production and marketing the documentary for sale for television release.

10. Contact Information

Peter Pepe
P.O. Box 185
Glens Falls, New York 12801
www.pepeproductions.com
Telephone: xxx-xxx-xxxx
E-mail: xxxxxxxxx@xx.xxx

Appendix 2
DOCUMENTARY TREATMENT

THERE ARE MANY DIFFERENT STYLES for writing a documentary treatment. The following is an example of how we approached our treatment for this documentary. The treatment has been edited for inclusion in this book.

Working Title (Subject to Change):
The Forgotten Confederate Privateer:
The Search for the Jeff Davis, *a Civil War Raider**

Treatment prepared by
Joseph W. Zarzynski and Peter Pepe
Pepe Productions
P.O. Box 185
Glens Falls, New York 12801
www.pepeproductions.com
April 2009

    The documentary opens at the office of the Lighthouse Archaeological Maritime Program, known as LAMP, in sunny St. Augustine, Florida. LAMP is a not-for-profit corporation, and its office is on the grounds of the picturesque St. Augustine Lighthouse & Museum on Anastasia Island, just south of the downtown area of the City of St. Augustine. It is morning and the LAMP team is preparing its gear and personnel, as the research team will be going out to a nearby offshore

Documentary Filmmaking for Archaeologists, by Peter Pepe and Joseph W. Zarzynski, 191–195. © 2012 Left Coast Press, Inc. All rights reserved.
* The final title for this documentary is *Search for the* Jefferson Davis: *Trader, Slaver, Raider.*

site to continue their ongoing underwater archaeological investigation of a unique, double shipwreck site. We see B-roll of the team loading up trucks with scuba gear and underwater archaeological recording equipment, and the LAMP field school members heading down to their research boat at a nearby pier. Narration introduces the LAMP crew of several archaeologists, students, and volunteers and explains what they are doing.

LAMP archaeologists are being interviewed and begin to tell the story of the brig *Jefferson Davis*, a feared Confederate privateer during the American Civil War. The interviewees relate the little-known story of the rebel raider and its maritime mystery whose origins date back to the days of the illegal trans-Atlantic slave trade of the mid-nineteenth century and into the American Civil War (1861–1865).

The privateer's structural remains have been lost for nearly 150 years. The vessel was lost in August 1861 after it grounded in the treacherous shallow waters at the bar off St. Augustine, Florida. Narration and interviewees begin to tell the story of the three careers of the fabled watercraft—the *Jefferson Davis*, sometimes referred to as the *Jeff Davis*. We see paintings and computer-generated still images of a sailing brig. Prior to its career as a rebel raider with a government license to seize enemy vessels and bring them up for condemnation and sale, the vessel had a lengthy commercial career. Built in Baltimore, Maryland, in 1845 as the brig *Putnam*, the craft was first employed as a commercial trader. Later, the watercraft even had a period as a notorious slaver, named *Echo*, engaged in the trans-Atlantic slave trade, which had become illegal in America in 1808. Maps show us the track of the careers of the *Jefferson Davis*.

The brig *Jefferson Davis* was one of the Confederate States of America's most successful and feared privateers, one of a small navy of armed private vessels that attacked Union shipping. We see animation of the privateer hunting down and then seizing an unarmed northern commercial sailing vessel. LAMP archaeologists, in interviews, tell how the wooden sailing watercraft had a short career as a Southern raider, only a few months' duration. Nevertheless, during that time, the first year of the Civil War, the *Jefferson Davis* prowled the eastern seaboard of North America, striking fear into the hearts of seafarers aboard ships trading with the Union. The *Jefferson Davis* seized nine prizes—three brigs, three schooners, two ships, and one bark. One of those prizes was the *S. J. Waring*. Aboard the prize was a small crew of privateersmen and an African-American steward named William Tillman. Contemporary newspaper lithograph images show Tillman. We see a reenactment of Tillman taking over the schooner. Interviewees relate the account of how Tillman killed several privateersmen to take back the vessel, and then he miraculously sailed it to New York City. We see one or more maps showing us the route of the Confederate privateer on its one and only cruise as narration tells its tale of success. One of the crewmembers of the privateer ship was J. F. Carlsen, who survived the sinking of the *Jefferson Davis* in 1861, only to be killed nearly three years later aboard the Confederate submarine *H. L. Hunley*, which sank in the Charleston, South Carolina, harbor after sinking the USS *Housatonic*. Narration explains this fascinating connection and Carlsen's story, as B-roll taken at the *Hunley* laboratory in Charleston shows us more about this sailor and the historic Confederate submarine shipwreck that was found in 1995 by Clive Cussler's team led by Ralph Wilbanks and then raised from the seafloor several years later.

After capturing nine prizes, the captain of the privateer *Jefferson Davis* decided to sail his vessel into the harbor of St. Augustine, Florida, a city with a populace sympathetic to the Confederacy. Instead, the vessel grounded on the bar outside the city, and the wooden watercraft was a loss and soon sank. Computer-generated images and animation show the demise of the famed raider.

It is now June 2009, and dedicated shipwreck scientists called "underwater archaeologists" are exploring a mysterious double-shipwreck site. Backed by archival research combined with solid scientific sleuthing, these underwater archaeologists are investigating an underwater cultural site, an unidentified ballast pile lying over sunken vessel remains. Computer-generated images and archaeological drawings depict the shipwreck site, as narration explains what is being seen. B-roll shows LAMP's scientific divers aboard a research vessel donning their gear and diving into the waters over the ballast pile site, and we view underwater footage of maritime archaeologists probing the site to uncover its secrets. One of the LAMP archaeologists being interviewed ponders, could one of these shipwrecks be the long-lost vessel, the Confederate marauder *Jefferson Davis*?

During the field school, the LAMP team—underwater archaeologists, students, and volunteers—are on-site conducting their fieldwork, a slow methodical process. B-roll shows the LAMP team onboard, and underwater B-roll portrays them at work around the shipwreck. Narration and LAMP archaeologists being interviewed explain how they are using science to test their hypothesis that this is the *Jefferson Davis*. Field school students are being interviewed, too. LAMP archaeologists being interviewed tell us what diagnostic artifacts and possible vessel remains need to be found to be able to prove it is the rebel raider. <u>Computer-generated images</u> and <u>photographs</u> of artifacts illustrate this.

Furthermore, we see <u>B-roll</u> and <u>photographs</u> of the research team members back in the LAMP compound and laboratory piecing together data to test their hypothesis. <u>Narration</u> explains what they are doing. <u>Interviews</u> of various members of the field school, conducted both in an office setting and onboard boats help explain the documentary tale.

Following LAMP's June 2009 fieldwork, the documentary shifts to forensic laboratories around the country where scientists conduct the laborious task of trying to solve the mystery of the *Jefferson Davis*. <u>B-roll</u> and <u>photographs</u> show these scientists at work. <u>Animation</u> of the *Jefferson Davis* is interwoven into the documentary. Using good old-fashioned science to determine the results of their archaeological investigation, the LAMP archaeologists are being <u>interview</u>ed to finally announce the outcome of their sleuthing.

<u>Shot List:</u> Possible B-roll and interviews, subject to change:

1. Charleston, South Carolina:
    a. B-roll of Fort Sumter from the battery
    b. Possible interview at the city's battery with LAMP personnel
    c. B-roll of the J. F. Carlsen head-and-facial reconstruction at the *Hunley* lab

2. St. Augustine, Florida:
    a. Interviews of key St. Augustine Lighthouse & Museum and LAMP personnel as well as some field school students
    b. Reenactment, using local talent, of William Tillman's takeover of the schooner *S. J. Waring*, with the production shot onboard one of the historic schooners in St. Augustine
    c. B-roll of reenactors on one of the historic schooners in St. Augustine, re-creating scenes of the *Jefferson Davis* at sea
    d. B-roll of Confederate reenactors firing cannon (tight shots) to simulate the attack on Fort Sumter (April 1861)
    e. B-roll of St. Augustine Lighthouse & Museum (lighthouse, offices, conservation lab, etc.)
    f. B-roll around St. Augustine (bridge, forts, downtown area, LAMP field house, etc.)
    g. B-roll of Fort Clinch on Amelia Island, Florida

3. Baltimore, Maryland:
   a. B-roll of Fells' Point area where the brig *Putnam* was built
4. Other sites to visit to be determined:
   a. Visits to laboratories where artifacts from the double-shipwreck site were sent, to conduct interviews with scientists and to shoot B-roll

Appendix 3
THE LOST RADEAU
VIDEO SCRIPT

VIDEO	AUDIO
•surface water with opening credits •lake and mountains, early morning •deploying side scan sonar towfish •water level, starboard side of boat	
•Zarr & Vince inside boat w/ sonar computer •diver gearing up inside boat •divers in water, safety check •underwater, diver descending	Mark L. Peckham: This is a touchstone of our experience with the French and Indian War. We have very few resources that survived from the French and Indian War period and this one is preserved and handed down to us three centuries later in pristine condition.
•historical signage, Radeau Warship •*Land Tortoise* drawing, plan view	Dr. Kathy Abbass: The twenty years before the American Revolution were very significant in the ultimate development of North America and people... people just are not as aware of that so the radeau is an interesting poster child for that if you will.
•uw B-roll of shipwreck	Dr. Russell Bellico: Just recognizing how old this is, how large it is, how intact it is. There's nothing else like this that you can see underwater.
•uw B-roll of shipwreck •diver descending to radeau •uw B-roll of shipwreck	Vince Capone: People believe that time travel is impossible. I say it is. When you dive on the radeau, you're literally transported back in time over 200 years. You are looking at a vessel that is the only remaining example of that class of vessel in the world – totally intact like the day it sunk. There are no other examples of this warship in the world. None that are close to bringing us back to that time in history. This... this is a time machine. It is a time capsule. It is a one of a kind in the world.

Figure A3: This is the first page of the editing script for *The Lost Radeau: North America's Oldest Intact Warship.* Note that the two-column format shows both the video and audio for the documentary (*credit: Peter Pepe*).

Documentary Filmmaking for Archaeologists, by Peter Pepe and Joseph W. Zarzynski, 196. © 2012 Left Coast Press, Inc. All rights reserved.

Appendix 4
SIMPLIFIED
SAMPLE BUDGET OUTLINE

For Pepe Productions' 2012 Proposal to a Major Television Channel to Fund the Television Special Entitled "Thresher—Oceanography's Sputnik"

I. General Expenses		
a) Production company—Pepe Productions		
1. Producer(s)	Principal Producer	$25,000
	Secondary Producer	$20,000
2. Director		$12,500
3. Other	Sonar Consultant	$ 7,000
b) Transportation		
1. Travel costs (air travel)	Europe & USA	$6,000
2. Vehicular costs	Mileage POV USA	$3,625
3. Vessel costs	Surface vessels	$2,000
c) Legal		
1. Contracts, releases, etc.	Bundle Legal Expenses	$2,000
2. Rights		
3. Copyright		
d) Insurance		$1,800
1. Office and equipment		
2. Errors & Omissions		
3. Liability		

Documentary Filmmaking for Archaeologists, by Peter Pepe and Joseph W. Zarzynski, 197–198. © 2012 Left Coast Press, Inc. All rights reserved.

II. Preproduction Expenses		
a) Research		
1. Researcher		$1,250
b) Script		
1. Scriptwriter		$10,000
III. Production Expenses		
a) Crew & equipment (if contracted as a package)		$14,500
b) Transportation		
1. Aerial vehicle rental (helicopter)		$850
c) Travel		
1. Rooms & meals		$2,000
IV. Postproduction Expenses		
a) Editing (video)		
1. Editor	50 hrs @ $125 per hr	$15,750
b) Graphics & special effects		
1. Animation	Animations	$8,000
2. Computer graphics, etc	Photoshop/Graphic Design	$2,000
c) Music		
1. Library music, rights		$1,000
d) Audio post-production		
1. Narrator		$2,000
2. "Sound sweetening"		$1,500
e) Online editing		
1. "Video sweetening"		$1,500
V. Distribution Expenses		N/A
VI. Contingencies		12.5%
Total Itemized Expenses		$140,275
Contingency Expenses 12.5%		$17,534
TOTAL PROJECTED EXPENSES		$157,809

GLOSSARY

ambient sound: The background noise of your surroundings.

analog (also analogue) signals: Audio or video signals translated into electronic pulses of varying amplitudes, as opposed to digital signals, which are translated into binary format (zero or one) where each bit is representative of two distinct amplitudes.

animation: A rapid display of images that creates the illusion of motion.

aspect ratio: The ratio of the width of the image screen to its height. The old television screens had a 4:3 aspect ratio; today's wide-screen televisions have a 16:9 aspect ratio.

assembly cut: The first cut or editing of film or video footage in a movie or documentary production.

Betamax (or Beta): An analog videocassette format that was a rival of the VHS format.

big screen: A nickname for movies.

blogs: Personal journals or columns published on the Internet (derived from "web log").

Blu-ray: A format that is gradually replacing the popular DVD format for some movie and documentary productions. Its name, Blu-ray, comes from the "blue laser" that is used to read the disc. It holds 50 GB of storage, about six times the storage capacity of a DVD.

bonus selection: An addition to many DVD and Blu-ray disc products that complements the feature film or documentary. Examples of bonus selections might be "The Making of the Documentary," "Interview with the Director," or "Outtakes."

boom operator: One of the most recognizable crewmembers on a documentary project, the boom operator's job is to maintain the microphone that is placed at the end of a boom pole and held closely to an actor or a person being interviewed. The boom pole is kept out of the view of the camera frame. This crewmember assists the production sound mixer.

brand: A name, design, logo, or quality that identifies a seller's service or product in a way that assists in marketing that service or product.

B-roll: Supplemental film or video footage that is shot and later used during the editing process to illustrate what an interviewee or the narrator may be discussing; any documentary footage that is *not* the interviews, reenactments, or illustrations. The term's derivation dates back to the days of linear film and video editing when two source decks were utilized, an A deck, containing footage of the person being interviewed, and the B deck, containing footage to expand on what the interviewee was talking about. By using these two decks to supply the master editor deck, the editor could insert "cutaways" over the interview, and the use of dissolves between scenes was made possible.

camcorders: Video camera systems that include a camera as well as a VCR.

closed ending: A story ending that neatly wraps up all the loose ends of the plot at the conclusion of the production and leaves viewers with a clear understanding of exactly how the story ends.

cloud (or **digital cloud**): An evolving paradigm in the computer world that provides for on-demand network access to shared storage computing resources that are available through cyberspace with service provider interaction.

digital media: The different platforms by which people can communicate electronically.

digital natives: People, both young and old, who have grown up using digital technology to communicate and who understand this technology.

digital revolution: A popular phrase that refers to the changes in computers and communication over the past thirty years or more as a result of the societal change from using analog technology to digital technology.

director: The person who has creative control over a documentary and decides when, where, what, and how to shoot the production.

docs: A nickname for documentaries.

documentarian: A person who makes documentaries.

documentary: A film, video, or television program that presents a subject in a factual manner using interviews, news footage, photographs, historical reenactments, and animation and is usually accompanied by narration.

DVD: Acronym for digital versatile disc or digital video disc. The DVD has enough capacity to hold movies and other multimedia presentations of audio and video. Most DVDs hold 4.7 GB but can hold up to 8.5 GB.

editing script: The script version used by the editor to edit the documentary during postproduction.

electronic press kit (EPK): The traditional press kit but in electronic form on a CD, DVD, or sent via e-mail.

errors and omissions insurance (or **E & O insurance**): A type of liability insurance that many documentary filmmakers and their production companies carry to protect themselves against lawsuits that might arise owing to the content in a documentary production. Many studios, television channels, and distribution companies require such insurance to protect them from frivolous lawsuits.

ethics: A set of moral principles of right conduct.

executive producer: A producer in a documentary or a motion picture who plays an extremely key role in financially supporting the project but is not necessarily involved in the day-to-day process of the filmmaking.

fair use: A doctrine in U.S. copyright law that allows the reproduction of copyrighted material without permission if its use is to review, criticize, teach, comment, or parody the copyrighted work.

FCC (Federal Communications Commission): An independent federal agency charged with regulating radio, television, satellite, and cable communications.

film commission: An organization, generally a not-for-profit group often with local government support, whose mission is to attract motion picture, documentary, and television crews to come and shoot their media production in the film commission's locale. Film commissions work with production crews to help troubleshoot logistical and permit problems, promote the marketing of the production, and assist in other capacities to make the location where the production was shot a filmmaker-friendly environment.

film festivals: Cinematic galas that present screenings of motion pictures and documentaries. Documentarians strive to get their productions into film festivals, as they serve as excellent venues to promote one's documentary.

film forums: Organizations set up by motion picture and documentary devotees to support and screen an array of diverse films and documentaries, domestic and international, that do not fall easily under the label of Hollywood-bred. Film forums often screen indie films that attract an eclectic audience.

film stock: The film on which motion pictures (movies) are shot.

fine cut: The final assemblage of the audio and visual components of a documentary or movie.

flip book: An elementary and early form of animation in which a series of pictures placed on consecutive pages in a book appear to be in motion as the pages are turned quickly. Flip books were initially popular among children.

4:3 format (or 4:3 aspect ratio): The ratio of width to height used in twentieth-century television screens and computer monitors. This changed with the introduction of the 16:9 aspect ratio, used in what are often called wide-screen televisions and computer screens.

gaffer: The crewmember responsible for the design and execution of the electrical and lighting equipment.

greenlight: An expression meaning that a television channel or other commissioning group agrees to extend funding and permission to begin production on a film or video.

Handycam: The name that Sony Corporation used for its video camcorders in the mid-1980s, named so to emphasize the small, palm size of the camera.

hard drive: A data storage device used today for many digital video cameras rather than a tape or microchip.

HDTV (high-definition television): Video technology that offers greatly increased screen resolution over traditional television, producing a clearer and sharper screen image.

Hi8: A Sony camcorder that had improved recorder electronics, introduced after the S-VHS.

idea: The original concept for a documentary.

IMDb (Internet Movie Database): A well-known and frequently visited website (IMDb.com) that has information on motion pictures, television programs, documentaries, actors and actresses, production crew, and other visual entertainment topics.

independent filmmaker (or indie filmmaker): A filmmaker who does not work for a major filmmaking studio.

International Documentary Association (or IDA): A not-for-profit organization for documentarians based in Los Angeles, California, that serves to promote documentaries and the genre of documentary filmmaking.

Internet television (or Internet TV): The digital distribution of television programing via the Internet.

intertitles: An editing technique used in the silent film industry, in which filmed title cards were inserted at key spots in the production to describe the narrative and indicate character dialogue.

interviewee: A person to be interviewed in a documentary.

jib crane: A device sometimes used in cinematography that holds a camera on one end with a counterweight on the opposite end. The jib crane, mounted on a type of tripod, allows the camera to be moved vertically, horizontally, or along both axes to acquire dramatic film or video footage.

"Ken Burns effect": A type of filmmaking editing style that uses panning and zooming of photographs and still images, named after the award-winning documentarian who popularized this documentary editing style.

kinetograph: An early motion picture viewing box, essentially a cabinet with a window viewer, where a movie could be watched.

lavalier microphone: A lapel-mounted microphone that is either wireless or is connected by a microphone cable.

letterboxing: An effect created in a video production that has been shot in a wide-screen aspect ratio but is being viewed on a standard-width television. The wide-screen production is shown intact, but the television screen has a black bar across both the top and bottom edges.

location release: A permission form that must be signed by the owner of a property where a documentarian wishes to videotape.

logging (or **cataloging**) **footage:** The process of reviewing and labeling video footage, interviews, and B-roll according to their subjects.

material culture: The artifacts, buildings, structures, and monuments left by past societies.

montage: A filmmaking editing technique of using a rapid succession of images or different film or video shots, usually to convey a passage of time.

Motion Picture Association of America (MPAA): A trade association that advances the interests of its members and also administers the MPAA film rating system. The MPAA was founded in 1922 as the Motion Picture Producers and Distributors of America (MPPDA).

narrator: A person, generally professional voice talent, who delivers voice-over commentary for a documentary.

new media: Communication using digital devices such as CDs, DVDs, computers, smart phones, tablets, and other new technologies.

nonlinear editing (NLE): An editing technique that allows documentary editors direct access to any video frame so that the editing can be conducted by cut and paste in any order in the documentary production. This technique is available only with digital technologies.

NTSC (National Television System Committee): The television system used in the United States and most other countries of North and Central America, as well as in a large part of South America, and in some Asian nations such as Japan, Taiwan, the Philippines, South Korea, and some other Pacific rim countries.

Official Selection: The title or honor given to any film or movie that has been accepted into a film festival.

open ending: A story ending that leaves some threads of the story unresolved at the end of the production. Some viewers dislike this type of ending, preferring a closed ending, where all details have been clearly wrapped up.

P.A. (production assistant): Often an entry-level job on a documentary crew. P.A.s generally do the grunt work, such as running errands for the director and other principals, making sure that release forms are properly filled out and signed, photocopying scripts, and other tasks. Many documentary principals first started in the industry as P.A.s.

PAL (Phase Alternating Line): A television and video system used in parts of Europe, Africa, Asia, and elsewhere; different from NTSC or SECAM systems.

panning: A camera shooting technique of moving a film or video camera, often mounted on a tripod, horizontally across a scene, from one side to the other.

personal/video releases: One-page forms signed by people to document formal permission for a production crew to film or videotape them for a specific documentary project.

pillarboxing: The effect of having black bars on the sides of a video or television image, caused by viewing a 4:3 (or standard aspect) video on a 16:9 aspect (wide) screen.

pitch: A formal submission of a program idea to, in this context, a television channel or other commissioning editor. This usually includes a written proposal and treatment and then even an in-person visit to sell your program.

postproduction: The editing stage in documentary filmmaking production.

preproduction: The preparation stage for a film or video shoot. During this time, the production crew is hired, the locations for shooting are determined, permits are acquired, and other details for production work are finalized.

press kit: A folder or packet generally given to members of the media, which normally includes a news release and other information to promote one's documentary.

producer: The person who oversees the vision and broad administration of a documentary and often makes a financial investment into the production. The producer also hires personnel, coordinates the distribution of the documentary, and makes most of the major business decisions on a production.

production: In the context of this book, a nonfiction motion picture that interprets and tells a factual story.

production assistant: See **P.A.**

production music: Music created solely for use in television, radio, movies, and documentaries. It is generally used as background music and thus often denotes music without vocals.

production sound mixer: The head of the sound department for the documentary who is responsible for the selection of microphones, makes sure all audio equipment is ready for the shoot, oversees the operation of sound recording, and mixes the audio during the production stage of the documentary.

prosumer cameras: Cameras that are a cross between professional and consumer cameras. A prosumer camera has some automatic settings, a principal characteristic of consumer cameras, but it also has some manual features, too. Archaeologists wishing to record B-roll footage for inclusion in a documentary should use no lesser quality than a prosumer camera, as its picture quality is far better than that of consumer cameras.

rasterizer (or **image rasterizer):** A process for taking an image and converting it into pixels or dots for output onto film or, later on in history, to video.

reflector: A shiny piece of material, generally rigid, designed to reflect light to illuminate a person being photographed, filmed, or videotaped.

replication: The process of creating new discs from a glass master, which is created from analyzing the master file and fixing any flaws in data formatting. The stamper then stamps out brand new discs from injected plastic so the information is embedded into the plastic while the disc is being made. Replication is done in a clean-room environment.

rough cut: The stage after the assembly cut in the editing phase of documentary filmmaking. During the rough cut stage, the editing team puts the documentary into its right order and also edits with an eye toward proper structure, rhythm, and pace for the documentary production.

royalty-free music: Production music that is recorded and sold for use without the requirement to pay royalties per unit sold or for any set time period. It is often used in documentaries as background music.

scene: A division in a documentary that represents action between people on-screen in a single place.

script: The text of a theatrical play, movie, television program, or documentary.

SECAM (Système Électronique pour Couleur avec Mémoire or Sequential Color with Memory): A video and television broadcast system used in France, Russia, a few small countries in Europe, and many countries around the world that were former French colonies.

shooting script: The script used by the director to plan out what interviews and B-roll need to be shot during the production stage of the documentary.

shot composition: Part of the art of video camera work, which entails taking the time to set up the shot to make sure it is properly framed, that it shows the relationships among the elements in the frame, that it conveys the story you intend to tell, that the camera is not facing into the sun, etc.

shot list: A list of film or video shots that the director and his or her crew need to acquire for possible inclusion into the documentary.

Silverdocs: An annual international film festival and concurrent conference that screens some of the best and most talked-about documentaries of the year. It is held in June of each year in Silver Spring, Maryland.

16:9 format (or 16:9 aspect ratio): A screen ratio, width to height, that is commonly called "wide-screen" and is currently used in HD televisions.

small screen: A nickname for television.

social media: Technologies on the World Wide Web and mobile devices like smart phones and tablets that facilitate communication and interaction with others. Examples include Facebook, Twitter, Flickr, and Yelp, among others.

sound bites: Short audio comments, each a sentence or two, that characterize the essence of what speakers are trying to say.

sound sweetening: Enhancement of a documentary's audio to get the best possible sound.

storyboards: A series of drawings or sketches annotated with directional notes that serve as planning aids for the documentary crew, talent, and interviewees of a documentary during production shooting.

stretch-o-vision: An effect that occurs when a video from standard aspect ratio, 4:3 format, is stretched to a wide-screen (16:9) aspect ratio and, in so doing, distorts the image.

tagline (or **logline** or **strapline**): A one-sentence description of a documentary or movie idea or concept that conveys the "hook" of the story.

talent: A general term for any actors, actresses, or other specialists who might do some type of voice work in a documentary or movie.

"talkies" (or **"talking pictures"**): Early motion pictures that incorporated synchronized dialogue into films and soon thereafter rapidly replaced silent films in the motion picture industry.

talking head: A person being interviewed on-screen who talks at great length about a subject. Too much of this kind of audio and visual in a documentary, even from an accomplished screen personality, can quickly bore an audience.

tease: A letter or even a short video sent to a production company, television channel, or other commissioning editor to ignite initial interest in a documentary project proposal.

Technicolor: A widely used color process that was employed by many Hollywood movie productions in the early years of color movies.

test screenings: Early screenings of documentaries by select audiences, generally first held toward the end of a documentary's rough cut, to acquire feedback and constructive criticism. Often following test screening, documentarians will go back and re-edit the production based upon this feedback.

theatrical release: Release of a movie or documentary into theaters rather than on television or as a DVD for home video viewing.

3-D documentary: A documentary production shot using 3-D camera technology. The acclaimed 2010 documentary *Cave of Forgotten Dreams*, about France's Chauvet-Pont-d'Arc Cave by Werner Herzog, is an excellent example of a 3-D documentary.

time code: A sequence of numeric codes generated by an automated timing system which, in documentary filmmaking production, is used for logging recorded video footage and, later in the process, to find and edit specific shots, scenes, and interviews.

treatment: A narrative, generally several pages long, that describes the overall story and approach of the documentary or movie. It is normally used to sell the documentary to a production company, television channel, or a commissioning editor.

VCR (videocassette recorder): A twentieth-century electromechanical device that records and plays back television and video programs using magnetic tape in rectangular-shaped plastic cassettes.

VHS (Video Home System): A video format that was once popular for analog recording of video onto cassettes.

Video8: A video camera system popularized in the 1980s. It followed the introduction of VHS and Beta. One advantage of Video8 over VHS and Beta was its compact form, as Video8 camcorders were small enough to be held in one hand.

video pirating: The unauthorized reproduction of copyrighted video productions; pirated copies are either sold illegally or used for home video use.

video release: Sometimes called an "appearance" release, this formally authorizes a documentarian to use the video taken of the person who has signed the release.

video sweetening: Enhancement of the video quality in a documentary or movie by optimizing and balancing the color and lighting of the imagery.

voice-over: See **narrator.**

voice talent: Professionals who do voice acting or voice-overs for documentary productions and other broadcast media.

Withoutabox: An Internet website (Withoutabox.com) devoted to helping filmmakers submit their recently released movies and documentaries to film festivals in the United States and in other countries worldwide.

YouTube: One of the world's most popular Internet websites, which allows anyone to upload videos to share with the public; the website (www.youtube.com) was created in 2005.

zooming: An editing effect to focus in on still imagery, such as a photograph, in a way that gives a sense of motion.

zoopraxiscope: A device developed in 1879 by visual arts innovator Eadweard Muybridge, considered by many to be the very first motion picture projector.

REFERENCES

About.com
   2012   Television History—John Baird. Electronic document, http://
          inventors.about.com/od/britishinventions/a/JohnBaird.htm,
          accessed January 31, 2012.
Accredited Language Services
   2010   How to Make a Great Documentary Narration. November 17,
          2010. Electronic document, www.alsintl.com/blog/documentary-
          narration/, accessed February 22, 2012.
ADR Productions
   2012   Who Invented the Video Camera? Electronic document, http://
          adrproductions.wordpress.com/2011/02/07/who-invented-the-
          video-camera/, accessed January 31, 2012.
Atchity, Kenneth, and Chi-Li Wong
   2003   *Writing Treatments That Sell: How to Create and Market Your Story
          Ideas to the Motion Picture and TV Industry*. 2nd edition. Henry
          Holt and Company, New York.
Aufderheide, Pat
   2006   The American University. In *The Documentary Film Makers Hand-
          book*, by Genevieve Jolliffe and Andrew Zinnes, pp. 12–14. The
          Continuum International Publishing Group, New York.
Baird Television
   2012a Paul Nipkow. Electronic document, www.bairdtelevision.com/
          nipkow.html, accessed March 1, 2012.
   2012b Baird Television, Welcome. Electronic document, www.
          bairdtelevision.com/jenkins.html, accessed March 1, 2012.
   2012c Charles Francis Jenkins. Electronic document, www.bairdtelevision.
          com/jenkins.html, accessed March 1, 2012.
Bean, Shawn C.
   2008   *The First Hollywood—Florida and the Golden Age of Silent Filmmak-
          ing*. University Press of Florida, Gainesville.

Bellis, Mary
  2012   History of the Digital Camera. About.com. Electronic document,
         http://inventors.about.com/library/inventors/bldigitalcamera.htm,
         accessed February 26, 2012.
Bernard, Sheila Curran
  2007   *Documentary Storytelling: Making Stronger and More Dramatic Non-
         fiction Films.* 2nd edition. Focal Press, Burlington, Massachusetts.
  2011   *Documentary Storytelling: Creative Nonfiction on Screen.* 3rd edition.
         Focal Press, Burlington, Massachusetts.
Braun, Josh
  2006   The Producer's Rep. In *The Documentary Film Makers Handbook,*
         by Genevieve Jolliffe and Andrew Zinnes, pp. 328–331. The Con-
         tinuum International Publishing Group, New York.
Canemaker, John
  1987   *Winsor McCay: His Life and Art.* Abbeville Press, New York.
Capon, Ellen
  2006   DVD Distribution. In *The Documentary Film Makers Handbook,* by
         Genevieve Jolliffe and Andrew Zinnes, pp. 354–357. The Contin-
         uum International Publishing Group, New York.
Cutler, Miriam
  2006   The Music Composer. In *The Documentary Film Makers Handbook,*
         by Genevieve Jolliffe and Andrew Zinnes, pp. 296–301. The Con-
         tinuum International Publishing Group, New York.
Das, Trisha
  2007   *How to Write a Documentary Script—A Monograph.* Public Service
         Broadcasting Trust, New Delhi, India.
della Cava, Marco R.
  2012   Books, CDs, DVDs, Photos Going, Going . . . As Our Stuff Evapo-
         rates, into a Digital Cloud, the American Home is Being Remade.
         USA Today, March 16–18: A1–A2.
Dirks, Tim
  2012   The History of Film—The 1930s. Electronic file, www.filmsite.
         org/30sintro.html, accessed January 31, 2012.
Discovery Communications
  2012   Overview. Electronic document, http://corporate.discovery.com/
         our-company/overview/, accessed January 18, 2012.
Dixon, Wheeler Winston, and Gwendolyn Audrey Foster
  2008   *A Short History of Film.* Rutgers University Press, New Brunswick,
         New Jersey.
Education Resources Information Center
  1982   The Reshaping of an Innovation, 1970–1982: Final Report of the
         Appalachian Community Service Network to the National Institute
         of Education (June 30, 1982). Electronic document, www.
         eric.ed.gov/ERICWebPortal/search/detailmini.jsp?_nfpb=true&_&

ERICExtSearch_SearchValue_0=ED238399&ERICExtSearch_
SearchType_0=no&accno=ED238399, accessed March 1, 2012.

Encyclopædia Britannica
2012   Robert Flaherty. Electronic document, www.britannica.com/
       EBchecked/topic/209319/Robert-Flaherty, accessed December 1,
       2011.

Fast Company
2012   The Brief but Impactful History of YouTube. Electronic document,
       www.fastcompany.com/magazine/142/it-had-to-be-you.html, ac-
       cessed February 1, 2012.

Fulford, Robert
2000   Robert Fulford's column about John Grierson and the documentary
       (*The National Post*, October 3, 2000). Electronic document, www.
       robertfulford.com/JohnGrierson.html, accessed March 1, 2012.

Furniss, Maureen
2008   *The Animation Bible: A Guide to Everything—From Flipbooks to
       Flash.* Laurence King Publishing, London.

Gladwell, Malcolm
2008   *Outliers: The Story of Success.* Little, Brown and Company, New
       York.

Greenwald, Robert
2006   Outfoxed: DIY Distribution. In *The Documentary Film Makers
       Handbook,* by Genevieve Jolliffe and Andrew Zinnes, pp. 370–373.
       The Continuum International Publishing Group, New York.

Hampe, Barry
2007   *Making Documentary Films and Videos: A Practical Guide to Planning,
       Filming, and Editing Documentaries.* 2nd edition. Henry Holt and
       Company, New York.

History
2012   History Shows. Electronic document, www.history.com/show,
       accessed January 20, 2012.

IMDb
2011a Nanook of the North. Electronic document, www.imdb.com/
       title/tt0013427/, accessed October 15, 2011.
2011b Biography of Sergei M. Eisenstein. Electronic document,
       www.imdb.com/name/nm0001178/bio, accessed October 20, 2011.
2012a Biography for Auguste Lumière. Electronic document, www.imdb.
       com/name/nm0525908/bio, accessed March 2, 2012.
2012b Biography for Louis Lumière. Electronic document, www.imdb.
       com/name/nm0525910/bio, accessed March 2, 2012.
2012c Biography for Robert J. Flaherty. Electronic document, www.imdb.
       com/name/nm0280904/bio, accessed March 12, 2012.
2012d Dr. Leakey and the Dawn of Man. Electronic document,
       www.imdb.com/title/tt0842910/, accessed July 8, 2012.

2012e The Sea Hunters. Electronic document, www.imdb.com/
title/tt0446636/, accessed March 12, 2012.

2012f Plot Summary for "Nova." Electronic document, www.imdb.
com/title/tt0206501/plotsummary, accessed February 15, 2012.

2012g John Rhys-Davies. Electronic document, www.imdb.com/
name/nm0722636/, accessed January 16, 2012.

2012h The Sinking of the *Lusitania*. Electronic document, www.imdb.
com/title/tt0009620/, accessed February 6, 2012.

2012i Biography for Walt Disney. Electronic document, www.imdb.
com/name/nm0000370/bio, accessed February 6, 2012.

Jolliffe, Genevieve, and Andrew Zinnes
2006 *The Documentary Film Makers Handbook.* The Continuum International Publishing Group, New York.

Klein, Martin
1997 Side Scan Sonar. In *Encyclopedia of Underwater and Maritime Archaeology*, edited by James P. Delgado, pp. 384–385. British Museum Press, London.

Krinsky, Tamara
2011 Museum Piece: A Different Kind of Documentary Exhibition. Documentary.org, Fall 2011. International Documentary Association. Electronic document, www.documentary.org/magazine/museum-piece-different-kind-documentary-exhibition, accessed January 29, 2012.

Library of Congress
2011 National Film Preservation Board. Electronic document, www.loc.gov/film/index.html, accessed January 18, 2011.

2012 History of Edison Motion Pictures: Origins of Motion Pictures—The Kinetoscope. Electronic document, http://memory.loc.gov/ammem/edhtml/edmvhist.html, accessed January 24, 2012.

Lindenmuth, Kevin J.
2010 *The Documentary Moviemaking Course: The Starter Guide to Documentary Filmmaking.* Barron's Educational Series, Hauppauge, New York.

Magdael, David
2006 The Publicist. In *The Documentary Film Makers Handbook*, by Genevieve Jolliffe and Andrew Zinnes, pp. 332–337. The Continuum International Publishing Group, New York.

Massachusetts Institute of Technology
2012 Philo Farnsworth. Electronic file, http://web.mit.edu/invent/iow/farnsworth.html, accessed March 3, 2012.

Morgan, Keya
2004 Mathew Brady. Electronic document, www.mathewbrady.com/about.htm, accessed January 16, 2012.

Nakashima, Ryan
  2012 YouTube Refining Its Channels. Associated Press. *St. Augustine Record*, February 21, 2012.
National Geographic
  2012 About Us. Electronic document, www.nationalgeographic/, accessed February 2, 2012.
Newton, Dale, and John Gaspard
  2007 *Digital Filmmaking 101—An Essential Guide to Producing Low-Budget Movies*. Michael Wiese Productions, Studio City, California.
Nichols, Bill
  2006 What to Do About Documentary Distortion? Toward a Code of Ethics. Documentary.org, March/April 2006. International Documentary Association. Electronic document, www.documentary.org/content/what-do-about-documentary-distortion-toward-code-ethics-0, accessed February 20, 2012.
Noble, Vergil E.
  2007 When the Legend Becomes Fact—Reconciling Hollywood Realism and Archaeological Realties. In *Box Office Archaeology: Refining Hollywood's Portrayals of the Past*, edited by Julie M. Schablitsky, pp. 223–244. Left Coast Press, Walnut Creek, California.
Pritzker, Barry
  1992 [Reprinted 2004] *Mathew Brady*. World Publications Group, North Dighton, Massachusetts.
Public Broadcasting Service
  2012a NOVA. Electronic document, www.pbs.org/wgbh/nova/listseason/01.html, accessed January 20, 2012.
  2012b PBS Editorial Standards and Policies, Electronic document, www.pbs.org/about/media/about/cms_page_media/35/PBS%20Editorial%20Standards%20and%20Policies.pdf, accessed July 4, 2012.
Renfrew, Colin, and Paul Bahn
  1998 *Archaeology: Theories, Methods, and Practice*. 2nd edition. Thames and Hudson, London.
Rosenthal, Alan
  2007 *Writing, Directing, and Producing Films and Videos*. 4th edition. Southern Illinois University, Carbondale.
Rossi, Fernanda
  2005 *Trailer Mechanics: A Guide to Making Your Documentary Fundraising Trailer*. Magafilms, New York.
Schablitsky, Julie M., editor
  2007 *Box Office Archaeology: Refining Hollywood's Portrayals of the Past*. Left Coast Press, Walnut Creek, California.

Shapiro, Mark
    2010   The History of Camcorders (March 24, 2010). *Internet Video Magazine*. Internet document, www.internetvideomag.com/Articles-2006/112706_historyofcamcorders.htm, accessed February 1, 2012.

Solnit, Rebecca
    2003   *Motion Studies—Eadweard Muybridge and the Technological West.* Bloomsbury Publishing, London.

Stephens, Mitchell
    2012   History of Television, *Grolier Encyclopedia*. Electronic document, www.nyu.edu/classes/stephens/History%20of%20Television%20page.htm, accessed January 20, 2012.

Teague, Matthew
    2007   Icons: The Voice of God. *Philadelphia Magazine*. June. Electronic document, www.phillymag.com/articles/icons_the_voice_of_god/, accessed January 16, 2012.

The Archaeology Channel
    2011   The Archaeology Channel. Electronic document, www.archaeologychannel.org/, accessed November 29, 2011.

Vhstodvd.com
    2012   History of the VHS Video Tape. Electronic document, www.vhstodvd.com/history-of-vhs-tape.html, accessed February 1, 2012.

Wallace, Heather
    2012   The History of Nonlinear Editing. Sundial Media. Electronic document, www.sundialmedia.com/sait/articles/found_a/heat_f.htm, accessed February 22, 2012.

Wong, Winnie
    2012   Errors & Omissions & Rights, Oh My! A Guide to Protecting Your Film. Documentary.org, Spring 2012. International Documentary Association, Los Angeles, California.

INDEX

Note: Page numbers appended with "b" indicate material in boxes; "f" indicates material in figures; "t" indicates material in tables. Page numbers in italics indicate material in photos.

ABOUT THE AUTHORS

Peter Pepe

Peter Pepe, President of Pepe Productions, is a corporate and documentary video filmmaker from Glens Falls, New York. Originally a professional musician and entertainment manager, in 1978, at the infancy of video production, he began working for a video company in Queensbury, New York, learning the craft from regional video visionary, Earl Smith. Soon afterwards, Pepe created a weekly television series for a Glens Falls television station that promoted community spirit. He later became executive producer for two successful video magazines, one about urban firefighting companies and the other on decorative painting. Pepe has produced, directed, and edited hundreds of corporate training, safety, sales, and marketing videos for clients around the world. He likewise has made video productions for museums and visitor centers as well as produced television commercials and music videos. In 2004, Pepe began collaborating with underwater archaeologist Joseph W. Zarzynski. This team has made three award-winning feature-length documentaries on shipwrecks and underwater archaeology. Pepe and Zarzynski and their colleagues are now working on new documentaries related to archaeology, cultural resources management, history, and underwater exploration. When not making video productions, Pepe consults on multimedia presentations and social media networking for businesses and not-for-profit corporations.

Joseph W. Zarzynski

Joseph W. Zarzynski is an underwater archaeologist and former educator who lives with his wife, Pat Meaney, in Wilton, New York. A native of Endicott, New York, Zarzynski has a Bachelor of Arts degree from Ithaca College (1973), a Master of Arts in Teaching from Binghamton University (1975), and a Master of Arts from the University of Leicester in the United Kingdom (2001). In 1990, he directed the research team that discovered the 1758 *Land Tortoise* radeau shipwreck in Lake George, New York, that is now called "North America's oldest intact warship." Following the archaeological study of this deep water shipwreck under the direction of Kathy Abbass and Zarzynski, in 1998, this British warship was designated a National Historic Landmark, only the sixth shipwreck with that national recognition. Russell P. Bellico and he co-founded Bateaux Below, Inc., a not-for-profit corporation that studies Lake George shipwrecks, and Zarzynski serves as its Executive Director. He is the author of two books on underwater mysteries and co-author of two books on shipwrecks and underwater archaeology. He was one of the scriptwriters and co-producer for the Pepe Productions documentaries—*The Lost Radeau: North America's Oldest Intact Warship* (2005), *Wooden Bones: The Sunken Fleet of 1758* (2010), and *Search for the* Jefferson Davis: *Trader, Slaver, Raider* (2011). Zarzynski credits his success in documentary filmmaking to working with his dedicated colleagues at Bateaux Below and Pepe Productions.